For as the rain and the snow come down from heaven,
and return not thither but water the earth,
making it bring forth and sprout . . . ,
so shall my word be that goes forth from my mouth;
it shall not return to me empty. . . .

Instead of the thorn shall come up the cypress;
instead of the brier shall come up the myrtle;
and it shall be to the Lord for a memorial,
for an everlasting sign which shall not be cut off.

Isaiah 55

PREACHING WITH CONFIDENCE

A THEOLOGICAL ESSAY
ON THE
POWER OF THE PULPIT

BY

JAMES DAANE

Resource *Publications*

An imprint of *Wipf and Stock Publishers*
150 West Broadway • Eugene OR 97401

Resource Publications
An imprint of *Wipf and Stock Publishers*
150 West Broadway
Eugene, Oregon 97401

Preaching With Confidence
A Theological Essay on the Power of the Pulpit
By Daane, James
©1980 Eerdmans
ISBN: 1-57910-699-4
Publication date: July, 2001
Previously published by Eerdmans, 1980.

Contents

Preface

BOOKS about preaching are legion. Why then add another? Chiefly for two reasons.

First, most books on homiletics are either too cluttered with detail or too general to be serviceable as textbooks for sermon-making. Years of teaching homiletics have led me to believe that seminarians need to be taught the elemental features of the simple, basic, one-point sermon. There are more ways than one to construct a good sermon, and many textbooks on homiletics try to teach the student many forms of sermon construction. But given their workload, seminary students who try to learn a number of sermon structures end up not knowing how to use any of them well. The time to experiment with the more sophisticated sermon forms is after one has learned the basics of sermon construction.

Sermon-making is both an art and a science. Most seminary students ought to concentrate on the science and leave acquisition of the art until after they have acquired some pulpit experience. We grant the poet what is called poetic license, but the right to bend and break the rules of grammar and logic is only earned by conforming to and mastering the laws of both. A great writer may end a sentence with a preposition; a freshman in college ought not to.

The great artists who have painted and sculptured the human body first had to learn the science of physiology. In the same way, the fundamentals that govern the *science* of sermon-making must be learned before the spontaneous, creative instincts of the *art* can be exercised profitably. Hence, one reason for writing another homiletics textbook is to show the student how to make the basic sermon.

A second reason for the writing of this book strikes me as even more important. There are many evangelicals who have a high view of the Bible and are willing to do battle for it, but who have a very low view of the Word of God as proclaimed in the sermon. This is one of the strangest paradoxes in the church today: vigorous defense of the Bible as the Word of God hand in hand with low esteem for the preaching of that same Word to build up the church of Christ. Many preachers these days do not even like to think of themselves as preachers, much less to have others call them preachers. They think of themselves as "enablers" or "coaches" and wish so to be regarded by others. Bible study, small groups, and religious sharing are increasingly urged as the route to revitalization of the church, while faith in the pulpit fades and grows dim.

I am convinced that it profits a church little to have a high view of Scripture if at the same time it has a low estimate of the preaching of the Word. The situation which prevails today betrays a serious misunderstanding of the nature of the church and its proclamation. My concern about this is reflected in the relatively high proportion of space devoted here to the theological issue of the mystery and the power of preaching. No one is apt to do the hard work of acquiring the skill of good sermon construction without being convinced that preaching is supremely important for the life of the church.

*   *   *

I must add here a sincere word of thanks to Dolores Loeding for her secretarial assistance and to the many students who have sharpened my thought by challenging it.

— JAMES DAANE

CHAPTER 1

THE CURRENT STATUS OF PREACHING

FOR the most part, Protestants today have lost their confidence in the effectiveness of the pulpit. While Roman Catholicism is enriching its tradition of church and sacraments by a new appreciation for preaching, Protestantism is impoverishing itself by abandoning the one great asset of its tradition: faith in the proclamation of the biblical message.

This loss of belief in the need for preaching and its power has occurred even among those who confess the highest respect for Scripture. Evangelicals who combine a strict view of the inspiration of the Bible with a low view of preaching it fail to perceive the mysteriously powerful creative nature of the Word of God. This short book is written in the hope of helping those who are called to preach catch a vision of the Bible's own understanding of the nature of its truth. The truth the pulpit proclaims is mysterious and powerful. Unless those called to preach sense the unique nature of their message, they are not likely to retain any confidence that preaching is really worthwhile.

In recent years there has been a steady exodus from the Christian ministry. Some have left the pulpit for what they believe are more effective forms of ministry in the church. Others take up new positions selling real estate or used cars, or as financial agents and public relations personnel for Christian institutions. Among those who remain, many emit sounds from the pulpit which suggest that preaching is not the best recipe for the renewal of the church.

During the 1960s many deserters of the pulpit cried for action rather than words. They contended that enacting Christian truth in Christian deeds was far more effective than preaching it in the pulpit. They wanted to *do* the Word, not say it. Biblical sermons, they felt, were merely "words about words." And so they summoned the church to communicate the Christian message by living it out—in the ghetto, in the civil rights and peace movements, in the streets, and in the corridors of political power where decisions are forged and social policies shaped.

It was of course ironic that those who issued this summons to the church did it by means of sermons spoken from the pulpit. Only a sermon was powerful enough to cut the sermon down to size; and the only place from which the church could effectively be moved out of itself into the world was the pulpit itself. We can see in this a parable about the mystery of preaching. There is something about the sermon as the *form* of the proclamation of the Word of God, and something about the pulpit as the *place* where the church speaks to itself and to the world, which indicate that pulpit proclamation is so effective as to suggest the mysterious.

The loud calls of the 1960s for the communication of biblical truth through Christian action seemed radical only to those who were calling as loudly that "the primary task of the church is to preach the gospel"—adding that if the church did this faithfully it would have neither the time and energy nor the need to formulate social and political pronouncements and take the kinds of action being suggested. But it makes little sense to speak of the church's *primary* task if for all practical purposes it has no secondary task. The deceptiveness of the slogans about the church's primary task of course escaped the attention of those who did not want to notice it.

Happily, there is increasing evidence that the evangelical community is coming to a greater awareness that Christians cannot simply speak the Word and ignore the social conditions of those who hear. The recognition is growing that the biblical injunction to be doers and not merely hearers of the Word applies to the church corporately as well as to its individual members. More and more evangelicals are coming to see that corporate sins are as real as those of individuals.

Both the social activists who only want to do the Word, and the self-proclaimed traditionalists who only want to preach it fall into extremism because they fail to see that the preaching of the Word is itself an enactment of the Word. Neither side recognizes the mysterious nature of the biblical Word, a unique Word which can not only be preached, but also *done*. When the Bible speaks of "doing" the Word it stresses the very special character of its Word. And the one who preaches the Word from the pulpit is a doer of the Word no less than the one who works in the streets for justice and righteousness.

Unless people perceive the mysterious creative power of the Word and recognize that when it is preached it *does* things and *creates* people who become doers of the Word, their desire to preach the Word in the pulpit or to enact it in the social and political spheres of life will not long endure. Communicating the gospel through Christian action will become a fad unless one acknowledges the distinctive character and power of the Word. If the Word is impotent, there is no reason to believe that it will be any more effective enacted in Christian action in the streets than through proclamation in the pulpit.

Where is the vitality that marked the upsurge of the social and political activity in the church of the 1960s?

The wind has gone out of the movement. First it lost faith in preaching, then in Christian action. The loss in each instance stemmed from a loss of faith in that power of the biblical Word which makes it uniquely and mysteriously effective.

This absence of confidence in the proclamation of the Word has also come to characterize evangelical churches and their ministers. While evangelical ministers still mount pulpits, what they say there (and what they publish in books about church renewal) betrays their loss of faith in preaching. The report is out that the renewal of the church comes not by preaching, but by such activities as fellowship, prayer, and Bible study—especially in small groups—in which Christians share their personal love and concern with each other. The smaller the group, the more effective. Meetings in private homes are preferable to those in church. Sharing hopes and fears, faith and failure, is the new formula for the return of the Holy Spirit and the revitalization of the church. Instead of summoning their members to gather for hearing the proclamation of the Word as expressed in the historical experiences of Old Testament Israel and the New Testament church "in the great congregation," many evangelical ministers believe that Christians gain more from talking with each other about their religious experiences.

What is this but a substitution of one's own internal religious experience for that redemptive history of God's actions as recorded in the Old and New Testaments which every evangelical calls the Word of God? True, for many evangelicals this substitution of sharing for preaching represents no great theological shift. They have long heard little more from the pulpit than the minister sharing his own religious experiences and relating those of others. The only significant change is that small group sharing is more self-consciously regarded as a form of the communion of the saints, which is considered a more

effective means of grace than traditional pulpit proclamation.

The very terms "preach" and "preacher" have fallen
into disrepute. After announcing the text—the traditional signal that what is to follow will be a proclamation
of the biblical Word—the person in the pulpit declares,
"This morning I want to share with you. . . ." If this is an
act of humility, it is an ill-placed humility. It is an indication that the evangelical minister has lost his identity and
the evangelical pulpit its rightful function.

One commonly sees the evangelical minister pronounce a benediction on the congregation with eyes
closed. This, too, is an act of mistaken humility. Though
it may seem to be a sign of no more than a confusion between offering a prayer and pronouncing a blessing, it is
in fact another case of depreciation of what preaching is
and who the preacher is. When Jesus sent out the seventy
to prepare the way for his arrival, he instructed them,
"Whatever house you enter, first say, 'Peace be to this
house!' And if a son of peace is there, your peace shall rest
upon him; but if not, it shall return to you" (Luke
10:5-6). The pronouncement Jesus mandated there was
neither a prayer nor a pious wish. In contrast, many occupants of today's evangelical pulpits do not dare to pronounce peace and grace and mercy even on the "house-
hold of God."

A small matter, perhaps, yet it is a clear window on
how many Protestant ministers see their task and function. They share rather than preach, they pray for rather
than pronounce blessing, they labor under a crisis of personal identity, because they have no clear conviction
about the nature of preaching. They no longer see clearly
that the unique and mysterious nature of preaching lies in
the unique and mysterious nature of the divine Word.

Preaching has fallen on evil days because the sermon is regarded as just another form of human speech,

rather than a special genre. The preacher is just another Christian without any special authority; the pulpit (whether within the church or on those frontiers where the church addresses the world) is just another platform or lectern — sometimes (even worse) it is a private stage. And when preachers believe this way, they lack the courage to speak with authority and to bless. Since they do not see themselves as speaking with authority, they easily conclude that they have no special responsibility or calling. Eventually, they begin to wonder why they are in the pulpit at all. Hence the exodus of capable ministers from the pulpit, and the readiness of so many qualified seminary students to avoid the pulpit to serve the cause of Christ in some other ministry.

For this low view of proclamation not only undermines the ministry of the pulpit, but also the minister. Someone has aptly defined preaching as "the communication of truth through personality." For that reason the individual in the pulpit who does not understand the nature of the Word and its proclamation will experience a personal crisis of self-identity, uncertain of what a preacher is and does. What a preacher is and what a preacher's function is, are interrelated, and both derive from the nature of the Word preached. In a code word: the preacher is part of what is preached.

Paul reflects this peculiar and remarkable identification of the preacher and the message when he says, "What we preach is not ourselves, but Jesus Christ as Lord" and then adds "with ourselves as your servants" (2 Cor. 4:5). Paul did not preach himself or his own religious experiences, but Christ; and in preaching Christ he knew that he himself was part of the content of his message. This is quite different from sharing one's faith and religious experiences in order to bring people to Christ.

Paul's understanding of his reality as a part of the biblical message reflects the larger truth that the church is a part of the message it proclaims. This is evident from the Apostles' Creed, in which the existence of the church is included *as a part of* the faith the church confesses and preaches. The church does not preach itself; the church preaches Christ. But there is no possible proclamation of Christ without proclaiming the existence of the church, for in preaching Christ the church cannot avoid proclaiming that it is the Body of Christ. The church is so identified with Christ that a proclamation of Christ is unavoidably a proclamation of the existence of the church. Similarly, the minister's existence as a Christian is a part of the sermon (which is one reason preachers must make and preach their own sermons!).[1]

The crisis of the pulpit, therefore, goes beyond the individual preacher's self-identity to the church's faith and its very identity as the church. When the church no longer understands itself in terms of its faith, it no longer perceives the nature of its pulpit. For what the church was called into existence by God to proclaim is precisely what it is summoned by God to believe. The current crisis of the pulpit is, therefore, a crisis of everything that is meant by "church." Why? Because a person's existence and function as a preacher, and the church's existence as "the pillar and ground of the truth" and function of proclaiming that truth, derive their distinctive reality and function from the nature of the Word.

When the pulpit is on the decline, the church is on the decline. When preaching is in crisis, the church is in crisis. And both crises stem from a failure to understand the nature of the divine Word.

As I entered the pulpit one Sunday morning, a

---

1. In the church's proclamation of the gospel the church reflects its existence, just as preachers in their sermons reflect their existence as Christian persons. But the church no more preaches its experience (church history) than preachers preach their personal religious experiences.

small boy whispered to his mother, "There's God." After the service, the mother related the incident to me with obvious amusement. I, too, found it amusing. But reflecting on the incident later I was reminded of the mysterious words of Jesus, "He who hears you hears me" (Luke 10:16). In the sober light of these words the faulty religious perceptions of a small boy reflected biblical truth in a way that the amusement of his mother did not.

A preacher is not God, of course. This would hardly even need to be said if it were not for the amazing and mysterious truth that the preacher does sound like God, because the preacher speaks the very Word that God himself once spoke and still speaks through the human being in the pulpit. God is present in preaching; indeed, God himself speaks his Word in the church's proclamation and gives utterance to his voice in the voice of the preacher. The pulpit is, therefore, where the action is, the action that should be any person's—particularly the Christian's —greatest concern. In the face of the preaching event, common sense and intellectual sophistication must be laid aside. The congregation in the pews hears not only its minister, but its God. The child's naive mistake did include an understanding of the pulpit which eluded his more sophisticated mother.

Of course, what the pulpit is and what happens in it are known only to faith. Everyday common sense does not acknowledge that God is in the pulpit, that "he who hears you hears me." But without such faith, there is no reason to leave the comfort of one's bed on Sunday morning to go to church. Since many church members do indeed have no such faith, the result is empty pews. And if the person in the pulpit does not have such faith, the discouragement of those empty pews will soon contribute to the erosion of the resolve to remain in the pulpit. For no one has biblical sanction to remain in the pulpit without being able to say about the words uttered there, "Thus saith the Lord." That awesome claim can be made without presumption only by those who believe that God himself speaks his Word through the sermon. This high mystery is the mystery of the pulpit. Until it is again acknowledged, preaching will continue to languish.

Henry Martin Robinson's novel *The Cardinal* gives the vivid description of a young priest's first administration of the mass. The fingers trembled, the body perspired as the young priest contemplated in his hand what he regarded as the actual body and blood of his Lord. Protestants may dismiss such fear and trembling at the sacrament, but unless its own ministers regain a similar sense of mystery and wonder at the event of preaching, the Protestant pulpit will never regain the power and force it once had. The cool, nonchalant, even cavalier manner in which many Protestant ministers occupy the pulpit is a travesty on its sacred and mysterious function. The holy place in a Protestant church is the pulpit; for it is there that God is present and from there that he goes forth and is heard in the midst of the congregation.

God talks in and through the sermon. So little accepted is this idea in current Protestantism that the term "God-talk" has become shorthand for human efforts to talk about God. In all the concern about language among contemporary philosophers of religion and theologians, the question at issue is not whether God speaks his Word in the proclamation of the church, but rather whether any human talk about God can have any meaning or validity. After a brilliant analysis of the question of whether human language is capable of saying anything truthful about God, John Macquarrie concludes his book *God Talk* by saying that he hopes so.

Once modern philosophy decided that God cannot be present and active in human time and space and hence cannot be heard in the pulpit, it was driven to question whether human words have any applicability to God at all. The church today is so heavily under the influence of this kind of thought that it is deeply confused about the nature of its message and the function of its pulpit. For unless God-talk in the straightforward meaning of that term is possible, unless God can talk through the human word of the church's proclamation, the possibility that anything true and valid about God will emerge from the language of the pulpit is excluded. The power and mystery of the church's proclamation lie precisely in the fact that it can talk meaningfully about God because its proclamation is employed by God as an instrument through which God himself speaks his own Word. The contemporary preacher of the biblical Word may and should say, with the ancient prophet, "Thus saith the Lord," because the Word proclaimed is literally what the Lord himself says, and *continues* to say.

The sober side of "he who hears you hears me" is in the words that follow: "and he who rejects you rejects me, and he who rejects me rejects him who sent me." This word of Jesus is so amazing a statement that many preachers are tempted to treat it as an exaggeration made for effect or a poetic expression pointing to something other than what it literally says. To the consternation of some occupants of the pulpit—and to the consolation of others—both parts of Jesus' statement are literally true. In them lies the mystery of preaching, the mystery of its power and glory.

This awesome, mystery-laden view of preaching is not based on a single biblical text; it comes to expression in many scriptural passages. One might state the truth of this even more boldly: the whole of Scripture teaches it, since the Incarnation—God becoming man—means not only that the church is the Body of Christ but that its voice of proclamation is the voice of Christ himself. Demonstrating this larger claim does not lie within the purposes of this book, but we do hope to satisfy the reader that the truth of "he who hears you hears me" does not rest on a single sentence in Luke's gospel, but is grounded in and announced by many other biblical expressions.

What Jesus taught the seventy is echoed in what he taught the twelve apostles. On commissioning them, Jesus warned them of the adverse circumstances they might expect, yet they should not "be anxious how you are to speak or what you are to say." The reason he gives for the courage he commands is: "for it is not you who speak, but the Spirit of your Father speaking through you" (Matt. 10:19, 20). In fulfilling their vocation in the face of rejection, duress, even persecution, the apostles are not to worry about the manner or the content of their speech, for this will be determined by the Spirit of the Father speaking in them.

The mystery of an event in which a human being speaks God's words and God thereby speaks his Word through human words cannot be explained in human language without recourse to paradox. It is clear that both *what* Jesus says, and *how* he says, it point to the awesome mystery of the nature of church proclamation. And if we reflect on this mystery, it is not surprising that the *how* and the *what* of the apostles' speaking is reflected in the relationship between the words of Jesus and the Word of God. The words of Jesus recorded in this scriptural text are very human words, yet they are regarded by the church as no less the Word of God. Similarly, the church rightly takes the very human words of the biblical authors as the Word of God. The mystery of the presence of God's speech in the words of Scripture and the speech of the church is a reflection of the mystery of God's presence in Jesus of Nazareth. We claimed above that a proper understanding of church proclamation involves the very faith of the church; we may now go further to say that it also involves the church's understanding of the Incarnation and of the Scriptures.

"He who hears you hears me" also resounds in Jesus' statement to the disciples after his resurrection, "If you forgive the sins of any, they are forgiven; if you retain the sins of any, they are retained" (John 20:23). Roman Catholics and Protestants differ about the meaning of these words. Catholics contend that the church can actually forgive sins; Protestants that the church can only *declare* sins forgiven by God. By maintaining this distinction between the declaration of forgiveness and the act of forgiving, Protestants make actual forgiveness a matter of faith.

But in spite of this disagreement, neither Roman Catholic nor Protestant theology teaches that a mere person can out of his or her own resources grant the forgiveness of sins. Both believe that these words of Jesus to the apostles assert the presence and the actual speaking of God. In Roman Catholicism this divine action and speaking is defined in terms of the church, in Protestantism in terms of the proclamation of the church. Regardless of which is biblically correct, both are closer to the biblical truth than those in the pulpit who do not literally believe Jesus' words "he who hears you hears me."

Paul also expresses this conception of the nature of preaching. He writes to the Thessalonian church, "When you received the word of God which you heard from us, you accepted [it] not [as] the word of men but as what it really is, the word of God" (1 Thess. 2:13). The words in brackets have no equivalent in the Greek text, indicating that the translators had some difficulty putting Paul's thought into smooth English. But these difficulties have nothing specifically to do with the English; the original Greek is equally problematic. It is the same paradox we saw in the language Jesus used to allay the apostles' anxiety about how and what they should say under persecution. Here in Paul's description of the Word—as in the words of Jesus—human language articulates what must be said sufficiently for our needs, but in the process of articulation shatters the limits of human language.

About this text Jerome Murphy-O'Connor writes: "The conciseness of this phrase *logon akoēs par' hēmōn tou theou* makes it almost impossible to translate. In fact, it is a combination of two expressions, *logos akoēs,* 'word heard,' and *logos theou,* 'word of God,' that Paul has run together because of his message." He sees the translation problem here as a sign that God has spoken in human language and as a commentary on Paul's statement that the Thessalonians received his human proclamation of the gospel "not as the word of men but as what it really is, the word of God." "That word [spoken by Paul] has been received and welcomed by the Thessalonians," Fr. Murphy-O'Connor says. "Though spoken by men, it is not a human word: it is still God's word."[2]

The point is clear: the very human word of church proclamation is nonetheless a divine Word uttered by God. Yet the language in which the point is made is like that of the Scripture itself—ambiguous, paradoxical, contradictory. This characteristic of the church's proclamation of the Word of God is a reflection of the manner and content of Jesus' being the Word of God. For Jesus, who regarded himself as the Word of God, asserts that he speaks not of himself, but by the commission and power of the God who is present and active within him (John 14:10). The church's proclamation of him who is the Word of God is very real human speech and yet no less very real divine speech, because it articulates one who is in the language of the Nicene Creed "very God and very man."

Again, Paul says the members of the Thessalonian church have been "taught by God" (1 Thess. 4:9)—that is, through Paul's preaching of the gospel—and chosen by

2. *Paul on Preaching* (Sheed & Ward, 1963), p. 172.

God "from the beginning to be saved," having been called by God to this "through *our* gospel" (2 Thess. 2:13, 14). Paul did not regard the gospel as *his* gospel, except in the sense that he proclaimed it. In 2 Corinthians 4:17-20, Paul describes his proclamation of the gospel by declaring both the gospel and its proclamation as a "ministry of reconciliation," in which God is "making his appeal through us." In the preceding chapter (4:1-6), he declares that in his preaching the glory of God shines in the face of Christ. What are all these assertions but varied ways of saying "he who hears you hears me"?

This should be enough to convince anyone who honors the Bible that God himself is present and actively speaking his Word in every authentic pulpit of the church, whether occupied by the most extraordinary or the most ordinary preacher. The "he who hears me" dissolves the pride of the former and encourages the latter to remain in the pulpit. For the true greatness and glory of any preacher resides only in the fact that God himself speaks his Word no less through the worst as through the best of sermons and no less in the least known as in the most renowned pulpits. The secular world and the secular media—and their imitators in the church—may pay special tribute to prominent ministers, outstanding churches, renowned evangelists, successful missionaries, and prolific and profitable religious authors, but all this at best means nothing and at worst may be an abomination in the eyes of God.

The best ministers, churches, and evangelists, recognizing that God himself speaks his Word through the proclamation of the church, therefore do not say "I say to you," or "the Bible says," but "Thus saith the Lord!" In biblical thought what the Bible actually says can only be heard at the point where God speaks his own Word in and through the proclamation of the church. The Bible is indeed the written form of the Word of God. But the Word finds a higher expression in that personal form of it which takes place in the pulpit of the church, for the pulpit expression which is true to the written Word approximates more closely that Word which became flesh in Jesus Christ, because it is itself an expression of that fleshly, human form in which the Word of God is present in Jesus Christ. As such it is an expression of the "he who hears you hears me."

That God himself speaks through the preacher is not a recently discovered biblical truth, but rather a truth recently lost! The Reformation, as is well known, put the pulpit instead of the sacrament at the center of the church's life and worship. Avid students of the Bible, the Reformers were powerful advocates of the value of the pulpit and the need for preaching. Calvin wrote a commentary on every book of the Bible except the last, and he preached almost every day. It was preaching above all else that gave force and shape to the Reformation.

On this Luther and Calvin were in total agreement. Both had high views of preaching because both recognized that God was present and active in the pulpit. Luther said forthrightly, *"Praedicatio verbi dei est verbum dei"*—"the preaching of the Word of God *is* the Word of God." Calvin put it even more bluntly. He said that God "deigns to consecrate to himself the mouths and tongues of men in order that his voice may resound in them" (*Institutes,* IV, 1). Elsewhere, he describes the minister of the gospel as "the very mouth of God" (*Homilies* on 1 Samuel, xlii, 42). Karl Barth echoes this Reformation view when he says, "Through the activity of preaching, God himself speaks."[3]

During the Reformation preaching thrived. The pulpit was a powerful force within the church and in the secular community because the church and those in its

3. *Come Holy Spirit* (repr. Eerdmans, 1979), p. xiv.

pulpits were convinced of the "he who hears you hears me." If the church regains this conviction, this biblical view of preaching, its pulpit will again become a mighty force. Then it will also seize the conscience of the nation and arouse it to be either for or against the church. It is first of all the absence of this conviction in the Protestant church today—evangelical and mainline alike—which gives the sting to Robert McAfee Brown's remark that "the trouble with the church today is that it is not in trouble."

Pope Paul VI, speaking of preaching, once said "No other form of communication can take its place." Would that more Protestants today were as aware of the pulpit's potential! Peter Berger put it this way: "Strong eruptions of religious faith have always been marked by the appearance of people with firm, unapologetic, often uncompromising convictions—that is, by types that are the very opposite from those presently engaged in the various 'relevance' operations. . . . Put simply: Ages of faith are not marked by 'dialogue' but by proclamation."

The church will not become a disturbing and healing power again until it regains the biblical view that in the pulpit God himself is heard, in his Word, addressing the hearer. The Proclaimed is also the Proclaimer. This is the mystery of preaching and of its power.

CHAPTER 2

THE POWER OF PREACHING

THE reason for the contemporary loss of faith in the proclamation of the Word from the pulpit lies in the widespread depreciation of words today. Sermons are said to be ineffective simply because they involve twenty or thirty minutes of preacher-talk. The pulpit is a talk-place; words cascade from it onto the pew, but little or nothing seems to happen. The lives of the people in the congregation remain the same. The religious language of the pulpit may have a soothing effect on some troubled souls but it really changes nothing, and the next Sunday the same troubled souls hear the same soothing idiom of piety.

Words are puffs of air, mere sounds that die on the wind, lacking inherent power. Like broken arrows they never pierce reality. A secular mind does not believe that "prayer changes things." A merely verbal exercise, prayer has at best a subjective effect. It may ease a person's inner turmoil; it may make the praying person feel better. But the personal realities of his or her life remain unchanged. To be sure, ministers serve a useful purpose when they strengthen the fearful, quiet the anxious, comfort the sick, and ease the exit of the dying. But all the multitude of words, however religious, leave the world as it was.

On this contemporary view words come to be regarded as mere symbols, meaning whatever their user wants them to mean. There is a famous passage in

Through the Looking Glass, by Lewis Carroll, which brings out this view of words in a vivid manner:

"When *I* use a word," Humpty Dumpty said, in rather a scornful tone, "it means just what I choose it to mean—neither more nor less."

"The question is," said Alice, "whether you *can* make words mean so many different things."

"The question is," said Humpty Dumpty, "which is the master—that's all."

Contemporary life is full of examples of this reduction of language to our subjective determination. Seldom has it been so pervasively obvious as it was in the US Senate hearings on the Watergate burglary and cover-up. Witnesses uttered testimony so calculated to obscure the truth by shifting the meaning of words that those listening could not tell whether they meant one thing or its exact opposite. What human language seemed to mean one month could be declared inoperative the next—without any apparent sense that the truth had been betrayed in the process. Words were like x's in an algebraic equation, having no *inherent* meaning but only standing for what was determined by the composer of the equation. It is no wonder that for people today, disillusioned by countless cases like this, the power of words to communicate has broken down.

When the nexus between language and reality has been broken and words cut loose from their mooring and cast adrift, so that the meaning of language is up for grabs, everyone is eligible to be his own Webster. With the possibility of communication destroyed, the Tower of Babel is being rebuilt. We can communicate with each other only if the meaning of our words derives from their relationship to reality. Without such a common point of reference our words pass each other like ships in the night. When this occurs community breaks down, for community depends upon communication and communication depends on consensus as to the meaning of words.

"God bless you," we say when someone sneezes — the same God whom we invoke before and after political conventions. In neither case are the words seriously meant or intended to effect anything. Similarly most swearing and cursing these days is excused because nothing is really meant by it. The one who uses words this way writes it off as wholly innocuous by saying "I didn't really *mean* what I said" or "I hadn't even realized that I said it."

Where words are not regarded as having rootage in objective realities, but are subject to such meaning as the user sees fit to attribute to them, dishonesty and tyranny are just around the corner. Both the political tyrant and the ordinary petty liar know how to redefine language and use it for their own purposes. What Marxist Communists mean by such concepts as freedom and democracy is a vivid but by no means unparalleled case in point. To this assault on the integrity of language, the ancient conception, both biblical and nonbiblical, stands in sharp contrast. Among the pagans and the people of God alike, language was regarded as an instrument of power. Words were thought to carry an inner dynamic. They were related to reality, possessing a force that affects reality for better or for worse. A curse was thought to carry power, not just vent frustration or anger. The object cursed was really cursed; and if that object was human the one cursed lived with a persistent sense of fear and dread, sometimes haunted with such terror as to fulfil the curse by self-destruction. Primitive people did not curse and later apologize.

Pagan thought in ancient times was more given to cursing than blessing. Biblical thought, by contrast, obliged God's people to bless and limited the right to curse to God alone. Paul reflects this in his injunction to bless one's persecutors, not to curse them (Rom. 12:14). But notice that ancient thought, both biblical and pagan, regarded words as carriers of power which affected reality for good or ill. Words were thought to have such power over reality because they were grounded in reality.

The religious literature of the two great cultures that bracketed ancient Israel, Egypt and Mesopotamia, demonstrates that their gods were believed to speak with power. When they spoke, things happened. Their words released the energies of the divine personalities from whom they proceeded. For all the vast differences that distinguished the words of Yahweh from the words of the gods of Egypt and Mesopotamia, the Old Testament does present Yahweh in the same way, as one who speaks words laden with power. Yahweh's words carry power over reality because they not only *create* reality, but even overcome what sin has done to created reality, and thus recreate reality.

The Hebrew *dabar*—"word"—carries with it the dynamic connotation of "event." Words are events, hence the biblical warning against idle words (Matt. 12:36). The remarkable possibility that a word is an event stems from the Old Testament conception that divine words always release an energy that actuates what they say. Events occur because of the divine saying of them. The very strangeness of that sentence indicates that the purely *formal* character of language tends to break down—or, better, erupts—to reveal those dimensions that transcend mere verbalization. This is something that eludes those who (like many evangelicals today) hold to a theology which reduces truth to mere propositional statements, nothing more.

Because language is creative, the poet is allowed to break the rules of grammar (though not all of them and not completely) in the name of what is called poetic license. Similarly, a good sermon is always the enfleshment of a good logical outline, yet the preacher may break through the mechanics of a good logical outline.

(Unfortunately, this sermonic license is little understood and thus easily — and often — abused.) For the laws of grammar and the laws of rationality define what is or was or has been, but the Word of God — also as it comes in the sermon — is dynamically moving to *create* the new that will be. Words have evocative power. They can call things into existence, change the old, undo what was, bring forth the new. They can bring light out of darkness and joy out of tears. This biblical conception of the power of words should give pause to those ministers who contemplate leaving the pulpit and those seminary students who plan to avoid it entirely under the illusion that the activity which really changes the world lies in some other activity.

The massive biblical evidence that the Word of God is laden with power begins in the first chapter of Genesis. The Old Testament begins by saying that God created the heavens and the earth and then immediately proceeds to tell how. How was light created? Genesis says that God spoke and light appeared out of darkness! God said let there be light, and there was light. He called to the waters above and to the waters below to separate, and dry land appeared. God said let the dry land produce, and it brought forth trees. The whole universe derived its existence and reality from the speech of God.

Accustomed to the doctrine of creation, we may lose sight of what a staggering thought it is. From our human perspective to create anything takes some doing. In biblical thought the "doing" occurs in the "God said!" Speech is ordinarily directed toward a hearer. But when God created the world out of nothing by speaking, to what or whom was his speech directed? He spoke to nothing and nothing heard his voice and became something. God's creative speech was not a divine soliloquy, for there is a response — a response that is not God, an event that is not God. What follows "Let there be light" is "And there was light." What we have here is a divine speaking which creates the object of its speech. In biblical thought, God calls "the things that are not, as though they were" (Rom. 4:17, ASV). This biblical teaching about creation is a profound mystery, which the human mind cannot wholly comprehend, but it indicates the peculiar power of God's word. "By the word of the Lord the heavens were made," sang the Psalmist, "and all their host by the breath of his mouth" (33:6). Such power elicits our praise and wonder and worship. It does not submit to our comprehension.

The same dynamic power of the divine Word which created the world is expressed in the biblical account of God's creation of Israel. The promise of being the source of a great nation is made to an aging couple without children. God brings forth Isaac by the word of his power. Abram becomes Abraham and Sarai becomes Sarah, progenitors of the nation of Israel. Again, God is seen to call the things that are not — and then they are. In Old Testament language, God is the creator of Israel. He *calls* Israel into existence by speaking to nothingness, to what is not there, to the offspring of a barren woman and a man who had lost hope of ever being a father. Out of an old, childless woman and her husband whom Paul describes as being "as good as dead" (Rom. 4:19), the nation of Israel emerges.

Israel knew that it had been called into existence by the Word of God, and that its reality had its origin in the fact that God had called its name. This is given especially clear and memorable expression in the words of the prophecy of Isaiah. "But now thus says the Lord, he who created you, O Jacob, he who formed you, O Israel: 'Fear not, for I have redeemed you; I have called you by name, you are mine' " (Isa. 43:1). With reference to its exile in Babylon, we hear "I will say to the north, Give up, and to the south, Do not withhold; bring my sons from afar and my daughters from the end of the earth; every one who is called by my name, whom I created for my glory, whom I have formed and made" (vv. 6-7). "I am the Lord, your Holy One, the Creator of Israel, your King" (vs. 15; cf. vs. 21). "Thus says the Lord who made you; who formed you from the womb" (44:2; cf. also vv. 21-24; 49:1, 5, 15). "Hearken to me . . . you who seek the Lord; look to the rock from which you were hewn, and to the quarry from which you were digged. Look to Abraham your father and to Sarah who bore you; for when he was but one I called him, and I blessed him and made him many" (51:1, 2).

Israel's faith that its existence as a nation stemmed from God's creative Word is reflected in a familiar Psalm in which David reflects on his own origin. He says, "For thou didst form my inward parts, thou didst knit me together in my mother's womb. . . . My frame was not hidden from thee, when I was being made in secret, intricately wrought in the depths of the earth. Thy eyes beheld my unformed substance; in thy book were written, every one of them, the days that were formed for me, when as yet there was none of them" (Ps. 139:13-16). Here Yahweh's all-pervasive personal knowledge of David even before his substance was formed reflects the content of that divine Word which actualizes what it says through its creative, evocative power.

Numerous other illustrations could be cited to demonstrate that the Old Testament sees the word of Yahweh as powerful and creative — both word and event, bringing things into existence by calling them into existence.

This Word of God which created Israel and recreated — redeemed — Israel is the same Word the church proclaims. Of course, the church proclaims this Word as fulfilled in the New Testament, but it is precisely a *fulfilled* Word, not another Word. Can the church, the minister in the pulpit, speak that dynamic, creative, reality-evoking and reality-changing Word? Let us look again at the Old Testament.

In the Old Testament, humans are said to speak the Word of God. The prophets of Israel are described as the mouth of Yahweh (Jer. 15:19; Hosea 6:5), and they assert, "Thus says the Lord." They do not say, "Let me tell you something the Lord told me"; rather, they declare "Thus says the Lord," and then *they say it* as something the Lord says. Not "I'm going to give you a *human* version of the divine Word," or "I'd like to share with you my personal version or experience of the divine Word." On the contrary, what they say after "Thus says the Lord" they characterize as itself the Word of the Lord. There is no doubt that in Old Testament thought people can utter God's Word because God himself utters his Word through them. This constituted the prophets as prophets and accounted for the mysterious power of their office.

But even ordinary members of the people of Israel had no doubt that they could speak words which conveyed God's blessing. Isaac blesses his sons, both Jacob and Esau; and because of his sinfully induced blessing on the younger, that on Esau cannot supersede or overrule it. Jacob, on his deathbed in Egypt, blessed his own sons. Balaam's intention to curse God's people is turned into a pronouncement of blessing on them (Num. 22, 23). Moses prescribes a benediction on the congregation which is still repeated over three thousand years later: "The Lord bless you and keep you; the Lord make his face to shine upon you . . ." (Num. 6:24). The pious Israelites blessed each other on the way to the festivals in Jerusalem: "We bless you in the name of the Lord" (Ps. 129:8).

Such human blessings of other human beings were regarded neither as prayers nor as mere pious sentiments nor as a religious fare-thee-well. Their human act of blessing was regarded as a release of divine power, whose beneficent force acted on the recipient of the blessing for good. Indeed, the Israelites even dared to bless Yahweh (cf. Ps. 103), and in and through such a word of blessing, they were confident that something happened which made a difference: namely, God himself was truly blessed by them.

How, we may ask, can one person actually bless another? How indeed, can a person bless God, bless him so truly that because of his blessing God himself is blessed? Rationalistic minds regard this as folly; evangelical ministers may be uncomfortable pronouncing benedictions because this is too wonderful for them; and the frivolous person may reduce blessings to something offered after a sneeze. The people of the Old Testament, however, believed that human words can bless. Indeed, they believed that they were enjoined by God to use them in this way.

*   *   *

The New Testament confirms and extends the Old Testament understanding of the Word. Again God is seen as one who speaks a powerful, creative Word, and humans, too, are seen as able to speak that Word of God and actually bless and recreate and make old things new.

For the New Testament, of course, the central reality is that God speaks his Word in Jesus Christ. Mary wonders how a virgin can give birth. What happens, in the language of Mary, is "according to your word." Again, the divine Word speaks to an impossibility (that of a virgin giving birth to a son) but it works its powerful work within the shadow that fell over Mary. "The Holy Spirit will come upon You, and the power of the Most High will overshadow You; therefore the child to be born will be called holy, the Son of God" (Luke 1:35). By the power of his Word, God begets (creates, fathers, produces — words fail here) the incarnate Christ.

Christ is God's Word both as the instrument of revelation and as the actualization of revelation. He is both word and event, the embodiment of an actualization of

God's speech. Immanuel—God with us—exists because he is the Word God speaks.

Christ is more than a teacher merely imparting information. He is, as the Fourth Gospel says, the divine Logos made flesh. In early Greek thought *logos* did not mean "word," but rather the logical, rational order or structure which characterizes all of reality. It referred to the oneness, the unitive principle of multiple reality. Not until after the time of Homer did *logos* come to mean mere "word." When John employs the term in describing the Incarnation, he gives it a whole new dynamic dimension. The *logos* of early Greek usage differs from the Hebrew *dabar* and John's *logos* as the static differs from the dynamic. Logos as rational structure reflected the nature of reality as it is (that is, as the Greeks saw it). The *dabar* of the Old Testament and the *logos* of John are energy laden, a dynamic force that creates and recreates. John's Logos can *become*. "The Word became flesh and dwelt among us."

Jesus revealed God's Word both in words and in deeds. His words carried authority. His contemporaries testified that "he taught them as one who had authority, and not as the scribes" (Mark 1:22). His words were *works* of power. He brought good news to the poor, healed the sick, released the captives, made the lame walk, raised the dead, forgave sins, multiplied loaves and fishes, stilled the storm, and cast out demons. His word took form in his works, and his works were the externalized actualization of his word's internal power. The nature of the Word showed its power in the authoritative character of his words and in his works.

The power and glory of the incarnate divine Word are disclosed even more brightly in the cross and resurrection. Out of the silence of Calvary the divine Word takes all the mockery and hatred, the bitter rejection and brutal murder, and creatively, powerfully fashions the resurrection. Not apart from the ugly and demonic horror of the cross but *out of it,* God fashions the resurrection. The very word indicates that in a fallen world eternal life can emerge only out of death and the grave. At the beginning of time God created light in the realm of darkness (Gen. 1). Now through "the light of the gospel of the glory of Christ" he causes the light of eternal life to shine forth from the dark of the grave. "The God who said, 'Let light shine out of darkness,' has shone in our hearts to give the light of the knowledge of the glory of God in the face of Christ" (2 Cor. 4:4, 6).

The gospel, as the proclamation and preaching of Christ crucified and risen, loses none of this cross-and-resurrection dynamic power to overcome evil and to save. Hence Paul was not ashamed of the gospel, for in it is displayed God's power for salvation. Paul was determined to preach and to glory in nothing else, except Christ crucified. The power of the gospel made him want to preach also at Rome in order to achieve some results in the church there. Because of the inherent power of the gospel the proclamation of it would bring down the strongholds of evil.

The power of the Word is also apparent in the biblical teaching that the Word is able to make its own way. "So faith comes from what is heard, and what is heard comes by the preaching of Christ" (Rom. 10:17). The believing hearing of the gospel is effected by the Word. The Word itself creates its own hearing, as it once created its own world, by re-creating those through faith who once had no faith. Nothing more needs to be done; no homiletical gimmicks or artificial techniques are required to make the gospel effective. The gospel is mighty to work its way to those who have ears but do not hear. It breaks hearts of stone to create hearts of flesh. "Is not my word like fire, says the Lord, and like a hammer which breaks the rock in pieces?" (Jer. 23:29).

The Word of God can even speak to the dead, and the dead respond! Jesus cries with a loud voice to Lazarus to come forth, and a dead man hears and comes forth from the grave. The word of Jesus *creates* hearing and a living response in him. Nor is this an isolated incident: "The hour is coming when all who are in the tombs will hear his voice" (John 5:28).

Both of the above instances — the birth of faith and the hearing response of the dead — echo the earlier words "Let there be light" and that word of Yahweh which called a nonexistent people into existence. Both demonstrate that power of the Word to call things which are not as though they were — so that they then are. Jesus calls a dead Lazarus *as though* he were alive, speaks to him *as though* he could hear; and by the power of the Word Lazarus does hear and does come forth from the grave.

At Jesus' simple command "Go," demons departed from possessed men (Matt. 8:32). Through his word of forgiveness Christ obliterated sin, so that what was, was no more: " 'But that you may know that the Son of man has authority on earth to forgive sins' — he said to the paralytic — 'I say to you, rise, take up your pallet and go home' " (Mark 2:10, 11). At the rebuke of his word "Peace! Be still," "even wind and sea obey him" (Mark 4:41). The Word of God powerfully changes things: it creates compliance in demons; it frees a paralytic from a sinful past (contrary to the common notion that the past cannot be undone); and it creates a hearing even in nature.

"The word of God is living and active" (Heb. 4:12). How foreign to our rationalistic minds to imagine a word as *living* and *active!* In Acts 12:24 we read that the Word of God grew and multiplied. Again, how radically we must alter our habit of thought if we are to recapture the biblical idea of the nature of the divine Word! How much we need to listen with a fresh hearing to what the Scriptures say about the nature of its Word.

It is this Word—evocative, dynamic, creative, saving, sin-annulling, death-defeating, healing, life-giving—which the church proclaims. This is the Word the pulpit must preach, and those in the ministry are summoned by God to proclaim. Philosophers and politicians, the wise of this earth, the "best and the brightest"—none proclaims a message or speaks a word comparable to the Word the church speaks. For what distinguishes the speech of the church from every human word of wisdom is that in the voice of the church God himself speaks the Word by which the universe was created, redeemed, and set free.

Only in the church is the Proclaimed also the Proclaimer. It was to those commissioned to preach his Word that Jesus said, "He who hears you hears me, and he who rejects you rejects me, and he who rejects me rejects him that sent me" (Luke 10:16). This is the agony and the glory, the power and the foolishness, the high honor and awesome responsibility of the Christian minister. The Christian ministry functions on the borderline between the cross and the resurrection, between heaven and hell. This frontier is no place for the faint-hearted; those who have little faith in their message and its power do not belong in the pulpit.

The church must recapture this biblical view of its ministry and the Word it administers. When it does, it will become strong once again, able to preach in a way that will seize the conscience of the nation. Then Christians who once felt called to the ministry will be less inclined to leave it in frustration to become financial and public relations executives or psychiatric counselors or honest used car salespersons. Seminary students who are not in fact ashamed of the gospel will bear witness to it not only on college campuses, and in the ghettos, and in industrial and prison and hospital chaplaincies, but also in the parish ministry.

Wherever their ministry is—in a traditional parish or on the campus, in the clinic, or on city streets—those who are called to preach must function as preachers, not primarily as apologists or psychologists or sociologists. As a missionary, a minister may legitimately function in a variety of areas if commissioned by the church and always mindful of being above all a *minister of the divine Word*, a Word with something distinctive to say in every situation of life. If God's Word is so powerful that the demons and the dead and the forces of nature can hear and must obey it, then it can also work its own way and gain a hearing on the campus, in the clinic, and on city streets.

Called to preach, such persons must not hide their identity and calling as ministers of Christ. The power of the Word of God is not abstracted from the one who speaks that Word. As we have stressed, God's Word releases the power of God; therein lies the mystery and power of preaching. Thus no one called to preach the Word should lose faith in preaching. If preaching falls short of accomplishing what a person is after, there is no reason to believe that other forms of applying the Word will be able to achieve it.

*   *   *

What I have emphasized in this chapter was said by the prophet with power many years ago (Isa. 55:10-13):

> For as the rain and the snow come down from heaven,
>   and return not thither but water the earth,
> making it bring forth and sprout,
>   giving seed to the sower and bread to the eater,
> so shall my word be that goes forth from my mouth;
>   it shall not return to me empty,
> but it shall accomplish that which I purpose,
>   and prosper in the thing for which I sent it.

For you shall go out in joy,
and be led forth in peace;
the mountains and the hills before you
shall break forth into singing,
and all the trees of the field shall clap their hands.
Instead of the thorn shall come up the cypress;
instead of the brier shall come up the myrtle;
and it shall be to the Lord for a memorial,
for an everlasting sign which shall not be cut off.

The prophet's words vividly illustrate the power of God's Word. Like the falling rain and snow, the Word God speaks does not approach the earth and then make a U-turn and return to heaven. The ground is watered for the nourishment of our bodies; in the same way, the Word God speaks from heaven accomplishes what he intends. It will deliver his captive people out of Babylon with joy and peace.

God has identified his name and his reputation with the power of his Word. His willingness to be known and remembered forever by this efficacious power was the comfort and strength of Israel in its Babylonian captivity. Equally, it is the comfort and strength of those who preach and those who believe the Word of God today.

CHAPTER 3

THE INESCAPABLE OFFENSE

NEVER before has Jesus Christ been so widely presented to the sinner as someone who is "good for you." The potential convert is told that Christ will heal one's hurts, give one peace of mind and a positive attitude, help one be successful, and enable one to find personal fulfilment and realize all one's latent potential. In such preaching— and there is much of it among evangelicals today—Jesus is projected, as in Sallman's well-known portrait, as very attractive and appealing. Unconverted sinners are given the impression that if only they would give a little time and consideration to Jesus Christ, they would surely accept him as Savior. No hint here of Isaiah's stark portrait of one with "no form or comeliness . . . no beauty that we should desire him." Nothing about the possibility of being offended at Jesus. No recognition that Jesus "was despised and rejected by men," and was crucified by people who saw him firsthand because they were there.

No Christian would want to say that Jesus is *not* good for sinners. But it is clear from biblical teaching that one may say "Jesus is good for you" only within a context of recognizing that sinners can be and are in fact offended by Jesus. There is such a thing as the offense of the cross and the offense of preaching. Jesus offended people in his own day, and people are still in fact offended at the Christ. Indeed Jesus himself defined as "blessed" the person "who takes no offense at me" (Matt. 11:6).

32

Many of Jesus' contemporaries fell short of meriting that blessing. They were repelled by what he said. When Jesus taught that he was the food and drink of eternal life and that only those who ate of his bread and drank of his blood would have eternal life, "many of his disciples . . . said, 'This is a hard saying, who can listen to it?' " Jesus asked those disciples who murmured against him, "Do you take offense at this?" Indeed, they did, for we read, "After this many of his disciples drew back and no longer went about with him" (John 6:60ff.). The people who were closest to Jesus at the end, as the event of the cross neared, were offended by him. On the night of his betrayal Jesus warned his disciples that when God smote the shepherd the sheep would be scattered. That very night they would all be offended and flee from him (Matt. 26:30-31). Despite Peter's strenuous protests, that prediction was fulfilled only hours later.

As was predicted by Simeon in the temple, Jesus was for his contemporaries a "sign that is spoken against" (Luke 2:34). Yet in our day there are few who are offended by the message of those who present Jesus for their faith and commitment. In fact, those who preach the gospel make a studied effort to preach Christ in such a way as not to offend anyone. Some of those who present Christ as someone who is "good for you," even admit frankly that they do not tell their listeners they are guilty sinners. They justify this by saying that non-Christian people already feel guilty enough. Why increase their sense of guilt and self-rejection?

Those who present the message this way have learned from modern psychology that guilt and self-rejection are psychologically detrimental. (They do not recognize that what is psychologically detrimental may be religiously beneficial.) And so they often tell non-Christians that they ought to esteem themselves highly, and whatever their faults to accept themselves as they are, with all their warts and defects. Why should they have this kind of self-image and self-evaluation? Why should they love themselves? Because, they are told, God does! They are assured that God accepts them *as they are,* loves them *as they are,* and indeed so highly esteems them that he gave his only begotten Son for them. Surely God would not expend the life of his only and much-beloved Son for something of little or no value. What greater proof, then, that the sinner is acceptable, worthy of esteem, valuable, and lovable, than God's willingness to send his Son to redeem the sinner. Such a God is surely not one who would offend people. Such a Savior is surely without any qualifications "good for you."

*   *   *

Søren Kierkegaard contended that there are two concepts essential to a proper understanding of New Testament Christianity. One is faith; the other is offense. Kierkegaard, to be sure, understood this offense primarily in an intellectual sense: human reason is offended by being asked to believe that the eternal has become temporal, the infinite finite—and this can only be regarded as absurd to human rationality. However one may assess Kierkegaard's conception of the New Testament category of the offense, there is no doubt that he was right to insist that apart from the concept of the offense the message of the New Testament will suffer serious distortion, the very distortion seen in the contemporary presentation of Jesus as being merely "good for you." The Jesus that offends no one is not the Jesus of the New Testament; and if the proclamation of him offends no one, it is not the Christ of the New Testament who is being proclaimed.

In addition to Simeon's prediction to Mary at the time of Jesus' circumcision that the child being presented would offend many in Israel and the example of the fulfilment of this prediction when many followers left Jesus because of his claim that one had to eat his body and drink his blood to have eternal life, there are a number of other biblical passages in which the fact and nature of the offense become clear. Let us consider some of these briefly.

Matthew 11:2-6 records that when the imprisoned John the Baptist heard reports about what Jesus was saying and doing, he was led to doubt whether Jesus was in fact the Messiah for whom the Jews had waited so long. Disturbed, he dispatched some of his followers to Jesus to confront him with the direct question, "Are you he who is to come, or shall we look for another?" John apparently expected that such a direct question would elicit an equally direct answer from Jesus.

John's doubts are often explained psychologically as the expression of the depressed spirit of a man in jail. But the answer Jesus gives contains nothing to lift a mood of depression. On the contrary, Jesus answers John's direct question indirectly. His answer discloses nothing John did not already know; indeed, it only repeats the information that gave rise to John's doubt about Jesus' messiahship in the first place! Tell John, Jesus says to the messengers, that "the blind receive their sight and the lame walk, lepers are cleansed and the deaf hear, and the dead are raised up, and the poor have good news preached to them" (vs. 5).

But Jesus' answer contained one additional element, something John did not know. It was a warning: "Blessed is he who takes no offense at me." It was because John was in fact offended that he doubted that Jesus was the Messiah. When John had preached that the kingdom of God was at hand, he expected judgment. People should therefore repent and be baptized, because the Messiah would execute justice, put an axe to the root of the tree, and burn the chaff on the threshing floor. Instead, all reports about what Jesus was saying and doing bespoke love and mercy. His words and works were gracious: the blind were given sight, the lame enabled to walk, and the poor were hearing *good* news. That is why John was offended. Had Jesus executed judgment, he would neither have been offended nor in doubt that Jesus was the Messiah, even though he languished in prison. In short, John is offended because of the grace and mercy of God revealed in the person and work of Jesus.

Jonah is the classic Old Testament example of the same phenomenon. Called to go to the city of Nineveh to proclaim its imminent destruction, Jonah instead boards a ship for Tarshish. After Nineveh had been spared, he explains to God why he took flight:

> *When God saw what they [Nineveh] did, how they turned from their evil way, God repented of the evil which he had said he would do to them; and he did not do it. But it displeased Jonah exceedingly, and he was angry. And he prayed to the Lord and said, "I pray thee, Lord, is not this what I said when I was yet in my country? That is why I made haste to flee to Tarshish; for I knew that thou art a gracious God and merciful, slow to anger, and abounding in steadfast love, and repentest of evil" (Jonah 3:10–4:2).*

Jonah does not think God should change his mind about the destruction of a city. How far Jonah's attitude is opposite to God's is shown later when God explains that he repented of his announced intention of destroying Nineveh because it not only contained many people but "also much cattle" (4:11). What offended Jonah, what repelled him and drove him off to Tarshish, was the grace of a God who repents of evil.

In one of the parables of Jesus, a householder hires laborers at various times of the day, but when day is done pays them all the same amount. Those first hired are offended by this. The householder's reply stresses once more the priority of grace: "Do you begrudge me my generosity?" (Matt. 20:15; cf. RSV mg.: "Is your eye evil because I am good?").

Consider also Paul's teaching in 1 Corinthians 1, which opens up another element of the offense of this gospel. Paul says that the cross (and the preaching of it) is by human standards foolishness and a stumbling block. It is folly to the Greeks, who seek wisdom; to the Jews, who seek for signs and power, the cross appears as the ultimate weakness of God.

In biblical thought this offense is not mere annoyance because the herald of the gospel lacks personal charisma or eloquence, or speaks with a brogue, or has an unpleasant voice or distracting mannerisms. Every minister of the gospel should avoid putting that kind of obstacle in the way of those who hear his message. But the offense of which the New Testament speaks is far more radical and serious than any annoyance the preacher may elicit in the hearers. It is an offense that the *message* being preached arouses in the hearers.

The offense with which the New Testament is concerned is expressed in the passive voice. People *are offended*. Not that the hearer offends nor that the herald of the gospel offends. It is rather that the message of the cross of Christ arouses a reaction in the hearer, who is repelled, driven back, turned aside, or—in more contemporary idiom—"put off" by the gospel. Not that the message or Christ or the cross or the God of grace and mercy are themselves inherently offensive. None of these is in itself offensive. But when they are proclaimed they elicit the reaction of offense in sinful people. Sinful people are offended because they are sinful. They protest the goodness of God; they are repelled by his grace. In the language of the parable of Jesus, their eye is evil because God is good.

What precisely is so offensive about the gospel message that God was in Christ reconciling the world to himself? It is the fact that the Son of God had to die and to bear the full reality of hell in order that sinners might be saved. Sinners find it most unflattering that God had to do this to save people from their sin and its consequences. This hurts human pride and self-esteem. We are perhaps willing to admit that we are not perfect, that we have not always done what was right. But that we are so entrapped in the power of evil that deliverance can only occur by the death of the Son of God himself, and that we can have life again only if God himself in Christ takes death and hell and infinite destruction into his own experience—this offends us at the depth of our being. At this truth about ourselves we stumble and are driven back and repelled. We want no more of it.

Since all are sinners, all are offended in the moment of confrontation by the gospel. Their first reaction is that they find nothing good in this good news, and they reject the idea that "Jesus is good for them." Their attitude is the same as that of many in Jesus' day: "This is a hard saying; who can listen to it?" It is a task of faith to overcome the offense, and only faith can overcome it. Faith is accepting that the face of Christ was marred "beyond human semblance" (Isa. 52:14), that he had neither form nor comeliness, no beauty, but was instead "wounded *for our transgressions* and bruised *for our iniquities.*"

This function faith performs not only at the moment when the sinner becomes a Christian. Faith continues to overcome the offense throughout the Christian's entire lifetime. For as long as the Christian is also a sinner he or she is offended by the grace and goodness of God revealed in the Christ of the cross. Throughout all of life the Christian may sing "In the cross of Christ I glory," knowing that no one is ever free of those recurring occasions of being ashamed of the gospel and offended by the assertion that without that drastic action of God at Calvary there would be no hope and no future.

The sinner who is not yet a Christian and the Christian who is not yet free of sin cannot avoid regarding the gospel as something that is bad not good news, a message of judgment rather than grace and mercy. This reaction of the sinner not yet turned Christian and of the Christian not yet free of sin testifies to what the New Testament means by that offense which arises when fallen people are confronted by the gospel. But it also testifies to what the New Testament understands by faith—that which overcomes a person's first reaction to the gospel. The good news of what God has done for us is bad news until we admit what God has done *for us,* that it is something we needed more than anything else and could not have done for ourselves. Any presentation of Christ, any proclamation of the Word of God, in which no one is or can be offended, is not by biblical standards a biblical proclamation of the Word and of the Christ of the Scriptures. The Jesus who is *merely* "good for you," who does not offend the sinner, is not the Jesus of the Bible.

*   *   *

Any presentation of Jesus as one who is "good for you" without arousing within the hearer a sense of being offended is not, we have been saying, an accurate presentation of the Christ of the Bible. The Bible does not take a cool, detached, and nonchalant view of people as sinners. Nor will sinners who have heard an authentic presentation of the gospel have such a cool, detached, nonchalant view of themselves. The gospel will offend them even as it calls them to that faith which overcomes the offense, a faith in which they acknowledge that it is the very Jesus who offends them that is good for them. The same Jesus whom the Christian as a sinner finds offensive will in faith be acknowledged as the rose of Sharon, the lily of the valley, the fairest of ten thousand.

One way in which those who preach the gospel have tried to remove the possibility of the offense is to present the message in such a way as to suggest to the non-Christian that he or she is being presented with options. The sinner is thus led to think that a real choice is involved in which one is *free* either to accept Christ or to reject him. This gives him the impression, of course, that one has the *ability* either to accept or reject Christ, and that one has as much *right* to do the former as the latter. This is flattering rather than offensive. It enables the sinner to retain a sense of autonomy, the might and the right to say No to the gospel. Much that is said and done in most altar calls reinforces this impression of the gospel as something optional.

This of course is not the way the Bible thinks and speaks of the gospel. In biblical thought the gospel comes in the imperative mood. As Paul told the Athenians, "God . . . *commands* all men everywhere to repent" (Acts 17:30). One may indeed speak of the gospel as an offer of salvation or as an invitation to come to Christ and be saved. But neither the offer nor the invitation is an ordinary one. No person is free to reject the offer or to refuse to accept the invitation. The gospel demands that people repent and have faith in Christ. The Scripture accordingly speaks of the "obedience of faith," thus portraying faith as the response to a command (there is no obedience where there is no command); and the rejection of the gospel is regarded as a disobedient act that will not go unpunished. To say that in hearing the gospel the sinner is confronted with options to which he or she is free to respond at will is to speak of a freedom not unlike that of the citizens in a totalitarian state, who are said to be free to vote as they please but may end up in prison or exile if they vote the wrong way.

The gospel does not make faith an option. It demands repentance and commands people to put their faith in Christ; and it reinforces these imperatives by a threat of punishment for non-compliance. This offends the sinner only because he or she is a sinner. What Christian who gives the matter some thought would think of God as a loving Father if he did *not* command his children, whom he has created, to flee death and destruction but merely made it optional? Earthly, sinful parents do better by their children that that.

Those who preach the gospel as something optional preach a gospel that offends no one — except the God who was in the crucified Christ reconciling the world unto himself, whom it presents as nonchalant, callously uncaring about the welfare of those for whom Christ was crucified.

Furthermore, to present the gospel as something optional is to suggest to the non-Christian that the gospel is something that one can accept while yet a non-Christian — in other words, that acceptance lies within the resources which a sinner possesses. Such a presentation of the gospel will offend no one; again, it flatters the sinner and supports his or her self-estimation as autonomous, suggests that he or she has the right before God to remain a sinner.

Such a presentation of the gospel is not biblical. The Bible nowhere suggests that the non-Christian while yet an unregenerate sinner is able to make the most important and decisive religious decision possible, namely, the decision to believe and accept Christ. If the non-Christian is so spiritually healthy and morally sound that he or she can by an act of will decide for Christ and have faith in him, then that sinner is in rather good spiritual and moral shape. Nor is one in a critical condition if one is able to weigh the evidence and make the judgment that Christianity is true *before* becoming a Christian. Such a presentation of the gospel sinners would not find offensive, for although it suggests that they could use a "helping hand," it clearly implies that they do not need a divine Savior who goes through death and hell to meet their need.

*   *   *

It is common in many evangelical circles to assert that the missionary, the evangelist, and the occupant of the congregational pulpit must "preach for decision." Yet strangely and significantly this "preaching for decision" does not actually happen until *after* the sermon is finished in an "altar call." Many who proclaim the gospel make the appeal to their hearers to make a decision for Christ not in and through and by means of the preaching of the Word, but in the period that follows the sermon, using such means as lowering the house lights, asking that all heads be bowed and all eyes closed — not, as one might expect, for prayer but for hearing persuasive words and emotional appeals — while a choir may softly sing "Just As I Am, Without One Plea" (though the speaker is doing the best job of pleading he can) or some comparable song.

If ministers would *preach* for decisions for Christ, things would be better than they are. But is the elaborate altar call not really a denial that "faith comes from what is heard, and what is heard comes by the preaching of Christ" (Rom. 10:17)? Surely people who are converted should stand up to be counted and publicly confess their faith in Christ. But the effort to effect conversions in an altar call period after the preaching is finished would seem to be an unspoken, perhaps unconscious admission that one does not believe the preached Word has the power to convert and save. If faith, as Paul teaches, comes through the hearing of Christ preached, what more is needed? To think that more than preaching is required, that altar call must follow sermon to render the preached Word effective, betrays a lack of faith in the mysterious, creative, saving power of the Word of God, qualities which no other words possess, not even those well-intended human words heard in an altar call.

The church in our time needs nothing more than a renewal of faith in the power of the proclamation of the Word of God. A Word that works faith in sinners and saves them without their prior permission may offend sinners, and a Word that saves people through its human proclamation without additional words of persuasion and pleading may offend even the preacher of the evangel. But it is faith and only faith alone which acknowledges that character of the gospel which offends sinners; and faith and only faith which can overcome that sense of offense because it alone acknowledges that what a person is offended at is an echo of the grace of God, a form of saving judgment and a grace that alone can save.

What Christian would deny that he or she once resisted the gospel and was offended by it and still has moments which are not wholly free of such reactions? But if that is how things are, is "decision" the most appropriate term for conversion? Is the conversion experience not described more exactly by such terms as surrender to God and cessation of hostility and resistance to Christ — the attitude which confesses, "Nothing in my hand I bring" — not even my decision. Such a capitulation in faith more truly depicts the gospel's demand for obedience than does a presentation of the gospel which provides the sinner with options for decision.

CHAPTER 4

SOME PRACTICAL IMPLICATIONS

PREACHING, we indicated in the first chapter, is a mysterious event because God himself speaks in the proclamation of the church. It is also, as discussed in the second chapter, a very effective event because of the living, creative, power of the Word proclaimed, even though (as the preceding chapter stressed) it will always arouse the reaction of offense in those hearing for the first time.

If the nature of preaching is thus derived from the nature of the Word, certain practical considerations follow.

First, it is not the obligation of the preacher to make the Word of the sermon effective. The minister of the Word is called to preach the Word and nothing else. The Word is the power of God unto salvation. This divine power of the Word needs no human help to raise the dead or turn sinners into saints. It no more requires the assistance of sinful people — even sinful Christian people — to recreate the world than it needed human cooperation to create the world. Indeed, every human attempt, however well-meant, to make the Word of God effective and powerful to save is a presumptuous act of pride.

The Word of God is powerful enough to work its own way through the resistance of the human heart to achieve its saving purpose. Every attempt to empower the Word by human strategies and techniques is no less than gimmickry which dishonors the Word. The temptation to play God and make his Word effectual takes many and subtle forms. For example, to pray with (not *for*) an unbeliever, after one has preached the Word, in an effort to bring that person to conversion dishonors the Word and is a misuse of prayer, for the prayer becomes a human contrivance to accomplish what the preached Word did not. To unbelievers the minister of the gospel must preach the Word, pray that the proclamation will be effective, and then relax and let things rest in the hand of God.

It is not the duty of ministers of the Word to convert; it is only their duty prayerfully to preach the Word. Less than this they ought not to do; more they cannot do. Ministers of the gospel always bear in mind what Paul said; they may plant and water but only God can give the increase. This recognition of their limitations will not only foster an appropriate humility, but also keep them from trying to carry a burden they cannot bear. The achievements of preaching always remain in the hand of God.

But if the ability to empower the Word does not lie in us, it is within our potential, alas, to obscure and becloud the truth of the Word. We can place stumbling blocks and unnecessary offenses in the path that leads to faith in Jesus Christ. We can hinder the gospel's entrance into the human heart. Ancient Israel's ungodliness sometimes caused the name of God to be blasphemed among the nations. Preachers today can set up obstacles to the hearing of the Word in many different ways: by reducing the gospel to moralism, by self-righteous pride, by lazy sermonic preparation, by turning the pulpit into a personal stage, by bad grammar, poor speaking, disregard of logic. Unable to empower the Word, ministers can still make it difficult for others to hear the Word.

Another implication of the fact that God himself speaks through the voice of the sermon is that preaching must be a peculiar genre of communication, quite unlike any other form. Pope Paul VI, stressing the "supreme importance" of preaching, said, "No other form of communication can take its place." It is only in the sermon that the "Thus says the Lord" is appropriate. Only to those commissioned to preach did Jesus say, "He who hears you hears me." The church's proclamation of the Word is a unique mode of address. In it alone we have the biblical assurance that God himself speaks through the human voice a word that is "living and active," strong and mighty to make all things new.

The ministry today is in a crossfire. The faith of many ministers in their own ministry is corroded by doubts. If the pulpit is to regain its force and ministers their confidence in what they as ministers of the Word are doing, a deep conviction of the mysterious and powerful nature of the Word of God must be recaptured. Without this conviction, ministers can regard themselves as no more than "coaches" or "enablers" of their membership.

In this scaled-down version of the ministerial task lies the unspoken and erroneous assumption that the power needed to revitalize the church lies not in the Word but in the membership of the church. What was to be empowered is now regarded as possessing the needed power. With this the door is opened to preoccupation with the members' own religious experience; to religious sharing, in which one can of course only share what one has; to the effort to "raise the religious consciousness"; to the pursuit of the fruits of positive thinking and the exercise of "possibility thinking," by which one thinks religious possibilities into religious realities. All of these are as futile as the attempt to add an inch to one's height by thinking about it. Once the Christian ministry loses its vision of the *nature* of the Word, it is left only with subjective resources of internal religious experience, to be manipulated by all kinds of plans and programs, psychological techniques, and even gimmicks. All of them lack that one thing needed, that one thing which constitutes the distinctiveness of the divine Word—living, creative power.

Although the mystery of preaching will always elude exhaustive definition, and although God is indeed free to speak his Word in other ways than through church proclamation, it is necessary for the welfare of the pulpit to recognize that the sermon is a unique form of communication. It must not be confused with other forms of religious discourse. The sermon is not a religious essay. If this were recognized, fewer religious essays would be heard from the pulpit. Nor is the sermon a lecture, though many sermons are—to the greater boredom of the pew.

Furthermore, no matter how true it may have been of the apostles, it is not the case that the sermon of the preacher in the post-apostolic age is merely an act of personal witness. One can personally witness only to what one has seen, experienced, understood. A sermon as a proclamation of the Word of God is something more than mere personal witness, for the Word is always something greater than anyone's personal experience, appropriation, and understanding of the Word. Personal witness is always bounded by my experience of the Word, and the Word itself has no such bounds.

The content of the sermonic Word is not the preacher's own internal religious history but God's redemptive actions in objective history. It was Schleiermacher who led theology down the road of liberalism, contending that "preaching must always take the form of testimony . . . to one's own experience" (cf. *The Christian Faith,* pp. 245–348). In short, the sermon which proclaims the Word always says more than the preacher understands.

For these reasons preaching is not sharing. To be sure, the word *sharing* is much used these days to designate what goes on in preaching, and in many cases the word is aptly used. But to the degree that the sermon is sharing, not preaching, the pew is impoverished. For sharing, like personal witness, operates within the poor and meager limits of the preacher's own religious appropriation. One can only share what one possesses, nothing more. But what preacher *possesses* the Word? The preacher is called to preach the Word, which is always much larger, deeper, richer than one's personal appropriation of it. One can no more share the Word than share one's faith; such control of the Word is not given us. Note again that unless one acknowledges the inherent power and dynamic of the Word, one easily slips into the illusion that one has—indeed *needs*—power over the Word. Finally, the idea that preaching is sharing creates the theologically bad impression that a non-Christian can share in another's faith without personally having faith. The pulpit must not seek to share its faith, but call people to faith, which is something very different.

The sermon is a unique form of discourse because the Word it proclaims is unique. To equate the sermon with other forms of discourse is not only to commit a tactical error, but—far worse—to hide from the eye of the preacher the nature of the task of the minister of the Word of God.

CHAPTER 5

EXPOSITORY PREACHING

I F the preaching of the Word of God *is* the Word of God, as Reformation theology contended, then the sermon is a proclamation of the Word of God only if the *Word* is preached. In other words, a sermon is inextricably tied up with the Word. Without the Word, no sermon. If what the minister proclaims are human insights, however perceptive — mere human words even though they are pearls of wisdom — what is happening is not what the Bible regards as preaching. In the strict sense of the term, *authentic* preaching is expository preaching.

Exposition means a "setting forth." In expository preaching the sermon "sets forth" or "exhibits" the truth of the selected biblical text. Such preaching represents the assertions of the text in the form of a sermon. The sermon must say what the text says. Though using different forms and different words, it nonetheless only repeats (with illustrations and applications added) what the text has already said. The science or art of sermon construction has traditionally been called homiletics (from the Greek words *homo*, "the same," and *lego*, "to say or speak"). Thus homiletics is the technique of making the kind of sermon on a biblical text which "says the same thing" as the text says. The very word used to designate the science of sermon construction thus confirms the contention that all authentic preaching is expository preaching.

The word the New Testament uses for making one's confession of faith also suggests this idea of repetition, saying the same thing. The word for confession, as in Paul's statement, "if you confess with your lips that Jesus is Lord" (Rom. 10:9), is also *homolego*. To put it another way, the confessor hears the Word of God, believes this word, and *repeats* it with the mouth. This view of our personal confession of faith comports with the church's communal confession of its faith and its proclamation of the Word. What the church believes and what it preaches are the same. The church's proclamation of the Word is thus itself an act by which it confesses its faith.

Expository preaching is setting forth neither more nor less than the truth of the biblical text. In so doing the preacher is neither philosopher nor apologete nor systematic theologian. It is not required that the truth of the text be made simpler than it is or rationally transparent and comprehensible according to human standards. We can surely have knowledge of the biblical Word, but it is not wholly comprehensible to the human mind. No person can wrap his or her mind around the Word, containing it within one's mental grasp. And so a sermonic effort to make the truth of the text wholly rational by the canons of human logic betrays a lack of appreciation of the infinite dimensions of the biblical Word. The purpose of the sermon is rather to announce the message of his text, to herald the gospel, to proclaim the good news.

One consequence of this is that the preacher also need not personally comprehend the truth of the sermon entirely. The preacher is obliged to listen to the text, to know what it says, and to say it again, but not to understand it exhaustively or know how the truth of it fits in with every other biblical teaching or one's theological tradition. Not that one ought totally to disregard the rest of the Bible, nor one's theological tradition. Each of these in its own way will serve as a guidepost in interpreting the text. But one need not know the whole Bible, nor possess a final theology, before one is ready to preach on a given text. If that were necessary, what veteran preacher—to say nothing of a young one—would ever be ready to preach? The task of the person in the pulpit is to preach the Word, to *say again*—through one's own personality and language—what the Word says in the text selected.

To Christians in the first century the Apostle spoke with surprising emphasis about their knowledge of the Word: "You have no need that one should teach you; as his anointing teaches you about everything, and is true, and is no lie" (1 John 2:27). If every Christian knows the Word of God to this extent and thus does not need to understand completely every biblical text or every biblical book in order to have a true knowledge of God, this is no less true of the minister of the Word. The minister of the Word, knowing the Word, is relieved of the necessity of understanding every biblical text and every biblical book before being able and ready to make a sermon on his selected biblical text. For God's Word is a single Word. We do not speak of the Bible as the *Words* of God: God has a single Word, which comes to expression in every biblical book and in every text of every book of the Bible.

This being so, the minister is relieved of the unnecessary fear that one cannot faithfully preach the biblical Word without preaching on every biblical book and on every text of every biblical book. Because God has but one Word the preacher who preaches on any text knows that that sermon is an articulation of the one Word of God, since every text is not a part of the Word but a specific and distinctive articulation of that one Word.

Many in the history of preaching have tried to distinguish between expository and textual sermons. It strikes me that this alleged distinction is not based on a significant difference and hence confuses more than it clarifies. What is said to distinguish an expository from a textual sermon is the *number* of biblical verses on which it is based. Andrew W. Blackwood (in his *The Preparation of Sermons*) defines an expository sermon as "one that grows out of a Bible passage longer than two or three verses" and a textual sermon as one that grows out of one, two, or three biblical verses. He is not altogether happy with this distinction, because he recognizes that the two "often overlap." Nonetheless he accepts the distinction, supporting it by arguing that the shorter the text the more the preacher can seriously deal with the results of exegesis and—by contrast—the longer the text the more "you must select and omit, or else pass over lightly the results of exegetical study." Then comes the unexpected advice: "In expository preaching, therefore, put the emphasis on preaching, and not on exposition." The *non sequitur* is obvious: expository preaching becomes preaching which is not exposition.

Making a distinction between expository and textual preaching on the basis of the length of the text would thus seem to be an act not of discrimination but of confusion. True, it is often more difficult to preach on a long biblical passage than on a short one, but the degree of difficulty does not make any essential difference between an expository and a textual sermon, nor does it provide support for the advice that expository preaching "puts the emphasis on preaching, and not on exposition." A commitment to expository preaching is a commitment to exposit the Word of God.

But it is *topical* sermons, not expository or textual ones, which Blackwood asserts have outnumbered all the rest in the history of preaching. He answers critics of topical sermons by pointing to Chrysostom, who preached seven sermons on the death of Lazarus, one of which carried the topic "Excessive Grief at the Death of Friends," having as its announced text I Thessalonians 4:13: "But we would not have you ignorant, brethren, concerning those who are asleep, that you may not grieve as others do who have no hope." This text of course says nothing at all about Lazarus. What it does in fact assert Chrysostom dealt with, Blackwood says, in his "first few paragraphs." Had he fashioned his whole sermon on what this text asserts, it "might not have lived for fifteen hundred years." From the viewpoint of expository preaching Blackwood's claim is pure irony. It seems that sermons not based on a biblical text are the best candidates for immortality!

A topical sermon is sometimes described as a sermon that "flows from its topic." But does it? A topic is a subject, *but a subject without a predication says nothing.* Strictly speaking, Chrysostom's topic — "Excessive Grief at the Death of Friends" — asserts nothing, and thus gives no indication as to what his sermon has to say about grieving too much when a friend has died. The point is that a mere topic, a subject without predication, is an undefined concept. Too often, then, the sermon comes to say whatever the topic happens to mean to the sermon-maker. The sermon does not in fact "flow from the topic," but from quite another source. Only to the degree that the topic expresses a biblical truth will the sermon be a biblical one. This is axiomatic. The one who stands before the church announcing that the Word of God is about to be preached would do far better, and would indeed be more honest, if the sermon material were drawn *directly* from Scripture rather than from the preacher's own understanding of the biblical meaning of the chosen topic. A sermon that "flows from its topic" is one step removed from Scripture in method, and may be even more steps removed from the truth of Scripture.

There is nothing theoretically wrong with a *scripturally authentic* topical sermon. Ministers who preach sermons on such ecclesiastical documents as the Heidelberg Catechism, or even on an officially interpreted

Apostles' Creed, do indeed preach topical sermons. But such topical preaching is guided and enriched by the fact that the official statement of faith is a communal church production, usually with a long history, not just what the individual preacher has discovered in the limited time since last Sunday.

Moreover, preachers who select their own topics, even if these topics are utterly biblical, take upon themselves an almost impossible task. Suppose one should select such biblical topics for sermons as faith, sin, death, atonement, creation, anxiety, or hope. The announced intent of the sermon is to proclaim the meaning such a topic has in biblical thought. What busy minister is able to do this within the possibilities for study found in one week, or even two? Not even an unbusy minister — if there is such — can within a week or two of sermon preparation uncover all the peculiar nuances that *faith*, for example, has in the Bible. And biblical topics like those mentioned are so rich and so many-faceted that if one did succeed in uncovering them all, it would still be impossible to put them together in any kind of manageable unity.

Even the best definitions that theologians have given the biblical concept of faith, while providing a working definition of faith, filter out all of its startling biblical features, leaving a relatively bland statement of the kind one finds in the average systematic theology text. To preach such a definition of faith is virtually to insure that the sermon will be as bland as most people think systematic theology is. Most church members will hear what they already know and will not hear about those biblical elements of faith to which they have given little or no thought. The preacher is also hurt by this kind of sermon-making. There is in it none of the enrichment and growth that comes from working through the biblical concepts; and the sermon, made without excitement, is preached without passion.

Let us illustrate. According to the Heidelberg Catechism (Q. & A. 21), "true faith is not only a knowledge and conviction that everything God reveals in his Word is true; it is also a deep-rooted assurance, created in me by the Holy Spirit through the gospel, that, not only others, but I too, have had my sins forgiven, have been made forever right with God, and have been granted salvation." This is a very workable definition of faith. It points to certain biblical aspects of Christian faith. But let the one who would preach topically—that is, in a general way—about faith attempt to integrate the eloquent words of the catechism with the objective "faith once for all delivered to the saints," and integrate both with faith as the means of justification, and then take into account Paul's distinction between faith and works, and then do justice to what James says about faith without works, and add to that Jesus' designation of faith as a work, and put all these together with Jesus' statement to the blind man, "your faith has made you well" (Mark 10:52) and the words of the author of Hebrews that "faith is the assurance of things hoped for, the conviction of things not seen" (Heb. 11:1). Who is sufficient for these things—even in three weeks! What congregation could absorb such a sermon? Yet this is the assignment the preacher of a topical sermon on faith takes on when standing in the pulpit to inform the congregation what faith means in biblical thought—I say "inform," for such sermons can scarcely avoid becoming lectures or religious essays. And the task is even more unbearable for both the preacher and the congregation, if the preacher selects a less familiar biblical concept! There is nothing in itself wrong with an authentic topical sermon. Such preaching can, at least theoretically, be expository. But in terms of practical considerations, one wonders whether such topical sermons are possible.

If expository preaching means "setting forth" biblical truth (and it literally does), then all preaching should be expository. Limiting the term "exposition" to sermons based on a single verse or a few verses, and employing other terms for sermons based on larger biblical passages, creates confusion. It may also obscure the central fact we have been stressing: all authentic preaching is exposition of Scripture.

CHAPTER 6

CONSTRUCTING A SERMON

WHILE every sermon should be an exposition of a biblical text, this does not mean that the *structure* of every sermon must be the same. From the viewpoint of formal construction, there are several types of sermons. The message
of the text can be legitimately and effectively brought
across to the listener in a variety of ways. Sermons may be
constructed on the principle of contrast, on the dialectic
of question and answer, on a pattern of levels of meaning,
in which the sermon moves from one level of meaning to
progressive clarification of thought on deeper levels of
meaning. All these methods require considerable skill if
they are to be executed effectively. Such homiletical and
literary artistry is often beyond the beginning preacher.

Every good pulpiteer ultimately finds, through
experimentation and experience in sermon-making, a
particular style of preaching and sermon construction.
Such an attainment, years in the making, does not come
with a seminary diploma. Indeed, the wise preacher never
ceases to work on sermonic style. Still, art is long and life
is short, and one must begin somewhere. The wise student
will not begin with the more complex forms of sermon
structures or attempt to create an entirely new style of sermon construction. Rather, one should begin with what is
here regarded as the simplest and most basic sermon
structure.

More art than exact science, sermon-making is

harder to teach than mathematics and as difficult to learn as any art. Not that the demands of science can be ignored in acquiring the art of sermonic craftsmanship. No art is devoid of all science. There are certain laws of logic and thought to which deference must be paid if communication is to occur. To be sure, all artists will bend these laws to their own purposes—and bend them successfully. But one cannot ignore them. The poet may stretch the bounds of grammar and language itself for a particular poetic purpose. But poetic license may not be in disregard of all rules if the poet is to communicate something to others, and even a poet does not break the rules without having first mastered living within them. Every kind of artist must defer to the demands imposed by the message or idea to which he or she seeks to give artistic expression. For the sermon-maker this means that —for all one's need to be creative and right to change the rudiments of thought and language—one cannot, at the peril of loss of communication, ignore the fundamental rules.

We can illustrate this by an upside-down triangle. The vertex at the bottom represents the basic laws of thought and grammar used in ordinary speech. From this base-point the more artistic and sophisticated forms of communication may rise high and wide—almost without limit. But such flights of poetry, symbol, metaphor, image must retain an unbroken line of connection with the bottom point of the triangle. Retain this connection and more can be communicated than words can contain; abandon it and communication ceases.

There is at least one basic rule to which any type of sermon structure must yield tribute. *Every sermon must say one thing, and one thing only; and this one thing must be capable of statement in a single sentence.* This rule governs what we shall here designate "the basic sermon." To the degree that a sermon of whatever structure fails to meet this requirement, it fails in its purpose. The more points a sermon tries to drive home, the less it drives home. A many-pointed sermon makes no point; it only conveys confusion. If after hearing a sermon an intelligent listener cannot state its point in a single sentence, the pulpit has largely failed him or her. It goes without saying that if the preacher cannot give the gist of the sermon in a single statement, neither will the persons who hear it.

This does not mean that sermons should be shallow. Great truth can be simply stated. "God is love" is a simple statement but a profound truth. No doubt sermons that try to say many things will not fade from the pulpit, but they will continue to jade even longsuffering congregations. A great part of evangelical preaching is characterized by the lack of sermonic unity and integrity. The person in the pew has suffered many things on many Sundays from many preachers whose sermons are mere concatenations of discrete, unrelated religious comments held together by nothing but the sequence in which they are presented. Preachers seriously devoted to the Scriptures often deliver sermons whose various parts one tries in vain to put together in a meaningful way.

This should be a warning to seminary students and beginning preachers. Students who attempt within a few seminary years to capture the techniques and the craftsmanship of many kinds of structured sermons frequently leave seminary masters of none. Considerable evidence of this is laid publicly on the line every Sunday. Many of the sermons preached in thousands of pulpits across the country are not really homiletical *constructions* at all. If they were buildings, they would collapse before they were finished.

It would be misleading to give the impression that the task of constructing the basic-type sermon is easy. It is simple, in the way a sentence is simple compared to a poem, because it is nothing more than one of the elemental forms of communication. But even the simplest forms of good, clear, crisp communication are not easily come by. In fact few people communicate clearly, and those who do it well in either speech or writing have acquired and maintained that ability only by constant effort and alertness. Similarly, the construction of the simple, basic type of sermon is achieved only through hard work. Let those easily discouraged, however, remember that practice makes any art easier.

THE PROPOSITION

The actual construction of the sermon is preceded by a study of the materials out of which it is to be made. One must first select a text—"select" because the Scriptures themselves present no texts, only verses, and even the versification is no part of Scripture itself.[1] Having made the selection, one must study the text with all the exegetical, hermeneutical, and theological skills at one's disposal.

Not least, one must learn to *listen* to the text. Psychologically, this is very difficult. Every preacher must learn to recognize the danger of coming to the text with preconceived notions of what it says. Inevitably, one brings to the text whatever one possesses of a theological tradition, whatever shaped one's religious understanding growing up in a Christian home or attending Sunday School. More seriously, perhaps, one approaches the text with those theological definitions of biblical concepts learned in seminary, especially in studying systematic theology. No Christian can approach the Bible as though having absolutely no knowledge of it. No Christian comes to Scripture with a wholly open and uncommitted mind.

All of us, then, read the Bible with a pre-under-

1. Since the preacher must carve out the text, it should be referred to in the pulpit as "my" text—not "our" text. The minister, not the congregation, selected it.

standing and a pre-knowledge of it. Nonetheless, that understanding and knowledge, for all its essential truthfulness, is never without error, needing correction and a deeper understanding of its message. Hence we always need to listen anew to the Bible. As long as the Christian lives, as long as the preacher preaches, listening to Scripture is obligatory. In approaching a text preachers must allow the Scriptures to challenge and question their understanding of it. This kind of repeated listening and questioning is that fusion of art and science which constitutes sermon-making.

There is another subtle temptation to be avoided. The primary concern with which preachers often approach a text is a concern for "what it means for the hearer today." Eager to discover relevance, the minister never takes time to hear what the text really says. The desire to apply it takes precedence over hearing what it declares. Application dominates interpretation. Students are particularly prone to this folly — and folly it is, for how can one apply what one has not yet heard or understood?

Selection of the text, scientific study of it, and actually listening to it thus all precede the construction of a sermon. Only when the preacher has decided what the text actually says and is able to state in a propositional sentence what it declares can construction of the sermon begin. Otherwise, the preacher is not ready to restructure the truth of the text in the form of a sermon. Having heard the message of the text selected, a minister will be ready to go, and eager to construct a sermon, free to submit to, and to bend to the purpose of the sermon, those rules of logic and grammar which govern every form of human communication. One is then ready to construct the simplest, most basic sermon.

As hinted in the foregoing, the assumption behind the basic sermon is that every properly selected text expresses a truth which can be stated in propositional form.

Every text says something about something. When it is properly interpreted, its many elements, ideas, phrases, and clauses are seen to be interrelated in such a fashion as to express a particular primary affirmation. A given text may, to be sure, express more than one idea or truth. But every text makes only one *primary* affirmation. Thus the primary affirmation of John 3:16 might be summed up as "the greatness of God's love." But this familiar text also says other things: about the world, about the need for faith, about divine giving, and about eternal life. All these are secondary affirmations, not in terms of religious importance — the idea of God, for example, is surely a bigger and more significant idea than the idea of world — but in terms of *expression*, that is, in terms of what the text is saying. The important thing for the sermon-maker to hear is the text's primary affirmation, and this is heard when one understands how the secondary affirmations give content and definition to the primary affirmation. In John 3:16 the nature of the gift and the purpose and object of the giving all explicate and show the greatness of the divine love.

It is quite legitimate to make a sermon on any of the secondary affirmations of a text. There are a number of different sermons a preacher could make using John 3:16. But when one makes sermons on a secondary affirmation of his text, it ought to be in full awareness of what one is doing. Otherwise, one will fall into an erroneous interpretation, which fails to interpret this secondary affirmation in the light of the meaning of the text's primary affirmation. In such a case the sermon will say what the text does not say.

To say that a text says something about something is to say that the text has a subject about which something specific is said. In other words, it has a subject and a predicate; it makes a predication about something. In John 3:16 the subject is "God's love" and the predication is "greatness." Here we have the makings of a sentence or proposition: God's love is great. The subject of a text for sermon-making purposes is not necessarily the same as the grammatical subject. In John 3:16 "God" is the grammatical subject, but the subject in terms of what the text says is God's *love*. A clearer example, perhaps, is Hebrews 11:7: "By faith Noah, being warned by God. . . ." Faith is obviously not the grammatical subject of the text, but in terms of what the text asserts, faith is what the text is primarily about.

Again, the subject of a text is not necessarily its largest concept nor the one which seems most important to us. Here is a subtle temptation that sermon-makers must learn to recognize and avoid. God is a bigger concept than Noah, but in terms of the meaning of Hebrews 11:7, faith is the subject about which the text makes its primary affirmation. Our being saved (not perishing) might seem to us to be the most important thing John 3:16 is talking about, but it is *not* the primary concern and chief subject of this text. God's love is!

The advantages of preaching on a text which has been recast into a propositional statement are considerable. One not only makes a one-point sermon, but the point made is very specific and sharp. To preach about the greatness of God's love using John 3:16 as a text is not to preach *generally* about God; it is not to preach about the power of God or the mercy of God or the justice of God. It is to preach only about God's love. And not about God's love comprehensively and in general, but only about its greatness. It is to preach about God's love within the boundaries of the specific affirmation made in the predicate of the sermon's proposition. It is to propose sermonically no more and no less than does the sermon's proposition. It is to view and articulate the subject within the defined and limited focus of its predicate.

This concentration may frighten the beginning

sermon-maker. How could one possibly preach for a half hour or a quarter hour or even ten minutes on the greatness of God's love, or on the faith of Noah as expressed only in his building of the ark? Such fears, however, are dispelled as soon as it becomes apparent that adherence to this sermonic method forces one to probe deeply into the meaning of his text. If the text is John 3:16 one will soon discover that its truth is as deep as that love of God which gave his Son for the salvation of the world.

Indeed, if a text is regarded as the Word of God, it takes on depths of meaning and beauty and dimensions of such fulness as the human mind cannot fully grasp. The preacher who digs below the surface of a text to explore its depths will soon end up in the predicament of having more material than the sermon can contain. How quickly the beginning preacher, fearful of not having enough to say, becomes a preacher whose sermons are too long! And how helpful is this depth-probing of a text. Nothing will do more to help one become a solid and enriched biblical theologian. Superficial preaching on biblical generalities is profoundly detrimental to the preacher. The congregation gets little spiritual nourishment, and the preacher does not grow in an understanding of the Word.

A further advantage of the basic one-point sermon is that it enables a preacher to create sermons that are fresh and different every Sunday. Making sermons that present one specific point about one text prevents the preacher from preaching much the same sermon every Sunday. With rare exceptions every biblical text differs from all other biblical texts; even some which are verbally the same appear in differing contexts, and thus are not the same. No expository sermon on a biblical text may therefore be a simple repeat of a former sermon. Sermons that make many biblical points on a given text will soon be making those same points on any selected text. The preacher who covers too much terrain will soon traverse the same terrain again and again. Often in contemporary preaching the texts are different, but the sermons are monotonously the same. This criticism is frequently expressed with dismay by seminary students about the sermons they hear from the pulpits of their various denominations. They often find these pulpits boring and repetitious. No matter what the announced text, the sermon is the same. The fact will not go away: sermons which preach generalities are sermons which themselves become generalities.

The basic one-point sermon demands hard work of the preacher, but the rewards are great for both congregation and minister.

THE SERMON PROPER

By "sermon proper" I mean the body of the sermon minus what might be called the accessories (the introduction, application, conclusion, and illustrations). Its parts are those components in the text which come together to formulate and warrant the sermon's proposition (indicated by the roman numerals in the model outlines presented at the end of this chapter). Since this is material found in the text, it has therefore gone into making the proposition of the sermon. It is used in the sermon to explicate and exhibit the content of the sermon's proposition.

The sermon proper is not an attempt to prove or even argue for the truth of the proposition. It rather explicates, exhibits, spells out what the proposition declares. The components of this part of the sermon, therefore, must come from the text and not from anywhere else inside or outside the Bible. This constitutes an exposition of the sermonic proposition as it expresses either the primary or secondary affirmation of the text. What falls below each part of the sermon (the roman numerals in our model outlines) is in turn an exposition of that particular aspect.

Thus the whole structure of the sermon outline is determined solely by the text. The Word articulated in a given text determines what the sermon asserts; and as such the sermon says what the Word says. It is thus an authentic *homiletical* effort. In our example of John 3:16 (model outline #1), each roman numeral indicates some aspect of the greatness of the divine love, and the three divisions of the outline begin with "its." The use of this possessive pronoun indicates that what is asserted belongs to the divine love and is an aspect of its greatness. The headings which follow the roman numerals are not sentences; if they were, the sermon would lose its unity, for it would no longer be focused on what the predicate of the sermon's proposition declares about its subject. Each sentence would be a new and different affirmation, and the enumerated parts of the sermon would be as unrelated to each other as the items on a grocery list.

Note in the models given that an adjective appears between the "its" and the aspect indicated. Just as the predicate in the sermon's propositional statement specifies precisely what the text is judged to say about the subject, so these adjectives define each aspect of the subject more precisely. If the object of the greatness of God's love in John 3:16 is the world, that object is more precisely defined — with the result that the greatness of that love is more clearly indicated — if the world is further qualified by the adjective "unworthy" or "sinful." Similarly, if there was a reason for the great love God showed in giving his Son, one puts a clearer spotlight on that purpose by using the adjective "saving" or "salvific."

John 3:16 declares that God greatly loved the sinful world, so greatly that he gave his Son to the world, that through this gift of his Son, those who believe (in the literal language of the following verse, "the world") might be saved. What is here proposed is a simple, basic sermon that will express this fundamental truth about John 3:16. And this method can be used to elicit the fundamental truth of any biblical text on which we might preach.

To protect a sermon's function of saying again what the Word says, the introduction, illustrations, applications, and conclusion are not included in the formal sermon outline—no more than they are included in the sermonic proposition or the text itself. For these elements are not components of the biblical text. They are additions contributed by the sermon-maker—legitimately and necessarily to be sure, but nonetheless additions. Limiting the elements of the outline to what is derived from the text restrains the preacher from the temptation of smuggling into the very structure of the sermon material that is not in the text.

The introduction, of course, has to come first in a sermon; and the conclusion can only come last. Illustrations and applications may occur anywhere in the sermon, as the sermon-maker judges best. We shall treat these components in our final chapter. Here we stress that the distinction between these additions and the sermon proper, between what the text says and what the preacher says the text means, but does not actually say, must be maintained. The method of sermon outline and sermon construction suggested in this chapter would seem to safeguard satisfactorily the important distinction between what a text says and the preacher's own understanding of its proper application to the life of the hearers.

Before leaving this subject, we should avert a possible misunderstanding by elucidating further our contention that a text can be reduced to a propositional statement which must govern the sermon. The method of sermon construction advocated here does not arise out of a rationalistic understanding of the biblical Word. The Word which the preacher must proclaim cannot be reduced rationalistically to a completely logical outline and then to a sermon wholly restricted to these boundaries. Not that the Word of God is irrational or illogical: it is *more than* rational and logical.

This stems from the very nature of the biblical Word. That Word is not necessary, timeless truth, but a Word God speaks in his freedom, and, as stressed earlier, God's Word is not merely his speech but also his action. The Word of God bears the character of the historical. It is event, good *news*. Hence the Scriptures do not just present us with a compendium of true propositional statements, but with the truth in terms of history and by means of metaphors, images, symbols, parables, and poetry: and this comes to us through sacraments and by way of the mysterious event of proclamation. And so the sermon also makes use of symbols, illustrations, literary images. The Scriptures do not present all truth in conceptual terms; nor does the sermon have to.

The Word of God is larger than our power of comprehension. Its length and height and depth always exceed our grasp. It overflows our categories of thought, our logical structures, our definitions and explanations. The truth of the scriptural text will thus elude our best sermon outlines. Because of this transcendent dimension of the divine Word, the sermon always says more than the preacher knows and understands, and it may thus effect in the person in the pew changes and healings of the spirit of which the preacher is wholly unaware.

Because the Word eludes and transcends our efforts at absorption of it, there are no perfect propositional statements, no perfect sermon outlines, and no perfect sermons. Outlining one text will give the preacher more difficulty than the next, but none will be perfect. This inevitable limitation of even our best efforts to structure the thought of the text in unity and rational integrity is, however, no excuse for not making the effort.

We cannot exhaustively comprehend the Word of God, but this does not lead us to give up all knowledge of God. Similarly, we cannot capture the whole of the Word found in a single text in our outlines and sermons, but this should not lead us to give up on the effort to construct logical outlines and carefully worked out sermons. Preachers must recognize their limitations and take comfort and strength from the fact that God himself speaks his Word through our feeble and often faulty efforts.

The Word of God is not irrational. Although we cannot wholly comprehend the Word, we can have valid knowledge of it. A logical structuring of the Word, whether as done in systematic theology, in propositional statement, and in sermon outlines, is valid, indeed necessary.

But if the Word is not irrational, neither is it wholly rational, i.e., exhaustively definable in terms of rationality. God, Jesus Christ as the way, the truth, and the life, are more than rational and, in that sense, other than the merely rational. Therefore the truth the church proclaims cannot be wholly encapsuled in a system of theology, in a propositional statement, or in the structure of the best logical sermonic outline. Like a cup that runs over, the truth always overflows our logical constructs and conceptional thought. This reflects the fact that the *primary* purpose of the Word and its proclamation is not to increase our knowledge, but to lead us to the worship of God, whose components are both that wonder and amazement at God's grace which cries out "O for a thousand tongues to sing/My great Redeemer's praise," and that commonplace service daily rendered to God.

*　　　*　　　*

MODEL OUTLINES

Text: John 3:16:
For God so loved the world that he gave his only

Son, that whoever believes in him should not perish but have eternal life.

Proposition: The Greatness of God's Love (God's love is great.)

    I. Its Costly Expression

    II. Its Unworthy Object

    III. Its Saving Purpose

Text: Romans 1:16, 17:

For I am not ashamed of the gospel: it is the power of God for salvation to every one who has faith, to the Jew first and also to the Greek. For in it the righteousness of God is revealed through faith for faith; as it is written, "He who through faith is righteous shall live."

Proposition: The Power of the Gospel (The gospel is powerful.)

    I. Its Saving Character

    II. Its Divine Source

    III. Its Sequential Objects

    IV. Its Pauline Consequence

Text: Isaiah 55:6-9:

Seek the Lord while he may be found,
    call upon him while he is near;
let the wicked forsake his way,
    and the unrighteous man his thoughts;
let him return to the LORD, that he may have mercy
    on him,
    and to our God, for he will abundantly pardon.
For my thoughts are not your thoughts,
    neither are your ways my ways, says the LORD.
For as the heavens are higher than the earth,
    so are my ways higher than your ways
    and my thoughts than your thoughts.

Proposition: A Summons to Repentance
 I. Its Urgent Character
 II. Its Specific Content
 III. Its Compelling Inducement

Text: Romans 9:1-3:

I am speaking the truth in Christ, I am not lying; my conscience bears me witness in the Holy Spirit, that I have great sorrow and unceasing anguish in my heart. For I could wish that I myself were accursed and cut off from Christ for the sake of my brethren, my kinsmen by race.

Proposition: Paul's Anguish for His Brethren
 I. Its Sworn Verification
 II. Its Amazing Nature
 III. Its Un-Christian Object

Text: Genesis 22:1-14

Proposition: The Testing of Abraham's Faith (Abraham's faith is tested.)
 I. Its Provocative Antecedents
 II. Its Religious Nature
 III. Its Painful Execution
 IV. Its Unexpected Outcome

Text: Hebrews 1:1-3:

In many and various ways God spoke of old to our fathers by the prophets; but in these last days he has spoken to us by a Son, whom he appointed the heir of all things, through whom also he created the world. He reflects the glory of God and bears the universe by his word of power. When he had made purification for sins, he sat down at the right hand of the Majesty on high. . . .

Proposition: Christ: God's Final Word (Christ is God's final Word.)

    I. Its Earlier Expression
    II. Its Ultimate Form
    III. Its Eschatological Significance

CHAPTER 7

Starting, Illustrating, Finishing

THE INTRODUCTION

As the literal meaning of the term suggests, the introduction of a sermon must lead the hearers to the main point. An introduction that leads elsewhere is worse than none at all. Preachers use introductions because the hearer is, before the sermon begins, far enough afield from the sermon to need the prodding or rousing a good introduction provides.

There are various ways in which an introduction may ready the hearer for the sermon. Any kind of introduction is good if by direction or indirection it makes the congregation alert for hearing the sermon. The introduction may be a significant question, to which the sermon provides the answer. Or it may point out a dire need of the hearer, which the sermon intends to meet. The introduction may present a theme to which the sermon is the counterpoint. The method will commend itself to the preacher who truly believes that the message of the gospel is what eye has not seen, and ear not heard, what has not even entered into human imaginations.

To fulfil its function the introduction must be relatively brief, interesting but not too exciting; it must arouse but not retain the hearer's attention; it must be simple and not itself require explanation; it must be relevant but not highly controversial; it may be of biblical

73

origin but must not itself require interpretation.

If the introduction is dull, it will turn off the hearers before the sermon even has a chance. If it is too long, it will upstage the sermon. If it is too exciting, it will not let the hearer's attention go when the sermon proper begins. The preacher who introduces a sermon by a dramatic and abrupt announcement that he was up all night because his wife is on the verge of death can hardly expect the congregation to push this to a back road of memory when the sermon begins. Like biblical signs, sermon introductions must redirect the attention they arouse away from themselves toward the sermon. If the introduction employs biblical material which itself requires sermonic definition and explanation, it will become a sermonette, not a good introduction. Highly controversial political material is likely to overexcite emotions in the congregation and turn off the supporters of all political parties.

Though spoken first, the introduction is made last. The logic behind this is apparent. Sermons often change in the process of being made. Since the function of an introduction is to lead to something, the point to which the hearers are to be led must be determined first. Making the introduction last will protect the preacher from the subtle, often unrecognized temptation of allowing the introduction, rather than the text alone, to shape the sermon. Of course, no one begins the construction of his sermon without knowing the central meaning of the text. But as every experienced sermon-maker knows, one often comes to understand the text better in the process of making the sermon. This accentuates the wisdom of formulating last what will be spoken first.

ILLUSTRATIONS

A sermon illustration is not an end in itself. It must throw light on some aspect of the sermon and thereby clarify it.

Like the introduction and the conclusion, it must be subservient to the sermon; it has no independent value.

What constitutes an illustration? A story, a poem, a real-life happening, a reference to a current event, a quotation aptly put, a citation from a novelist—but always something that helps *illustrate* an aspect of the sermon. Illustrations are not injected into sermons to entertain the congregation or to display the minister's erudition. They should not be added to extend an overly brief sermon nor serve as a sort of seventh-inning sermonic stretch in one that is too long.

A sermon is not a shish-kabob skewer, alternating biblical meat with interesting anecdotes. If an illustration does not enlighten, it distracts, and an irrelevant illustration is worse than none; failing to clarify, it creates confusion.

Too many preachers tell too many stories that have nothing to do with their sermons. The temptation to become a raconteur or a comedian is something from which the preacher should flee. There are ministers whose brilliant sense of humor and professional's sense of timing would make them successful on the night club circuit. They make people in the pews laugh, but one wonders whether heaven is smiling. The Word of God is much too sacred for cheap embellishment. The preacher's talent, whatever it may be, must be subservient to the proclamation of the Word in the sermon. The pulpit is no private stage on which a preacher is free to exercise acting talents and thespian ambitions.

The point is not that there is never a moment in any sermon for a joke, a laugh, or an interesting story well told. But unless the illustration, of whatever genre, illumines some affirmation of the sermon it is intrusive. It hurts the sermon rather than helps it. If God speaks through the sermon, then humor should be used in a manner that comports with that fact. People do not come

to church to be entertained. God only knows the sorrow
and pain, the shame and hurt, the unbearable burdens,
shattered experiences, crushed hopes, and terrors of the
spirit which lie in the hearts of those whom the minister
faces on Sunday morning. Such human wounds are not to
be healed lightly, laughed off with the help of injections
of humor from a pulpit personality whose model is Bob
Hope or Woody Allen or Carol Burnette.

Judging whether an illustration is a good one, legitimately to be used in a sermon, involves the congregation
as well as the illustration itself. Illustrations that hit the
pew as new information have little illustrative power. Not
much light will be shed by allusions to Shakespeare or a
Dostoevsky if their writings lie outside the cultural ac-
quaintance of most of the persons in the pew. There are
exceptions to this rule, of course—as there are to almost
every rule governing the making of sermons—but in general, literary and historical illustrations that must be
spelled out and explained in detail are of little value to
the sermon.

Illustrations can also be found in the Bible. Here,
too, the rule holds: in order effectively to illumine biblical
material, an illustration taken from the Bible must be
simple and sufficiently well known as to require no exten-
sive explanation.

Anthologies of sermon illustrations are of very limited value. Even when they are not artificial and contrived, it is difficult to use these anecdotes without having
them sound artificial and contrived. The most prolific
source of good illustrations is real-life experience, the sit-
uations common to most of the people in the pew.

THE CONCLUSION

The conclusion of a sermon should be the easiest part for
the minister to construct. In an authentic expository ser-

mon the conclusion contains nothing new; it merely re-asserts the sermon's initial proposition. But it does so by drawing on all the richness that the body of the sermon has exhibited in the exposition of that proposition. It is characteristic of an expository sermon that its end returns to its beginning, because an expository sermon begins with its text and in its exposition never leaves its text. If the sermon-maker has listened to the text, and has come to know what it asserts before constructing the outline and composing the sermon, there will be no difficulty in formulating a conclusion which recapitulates what the text says and what the preacher has been saying through-out the sermon.

The concluding, capsule restatement of a sermon may take various forms. Whatever its form, the conclu-sion of a sermon must meet only the one requirement that it reassert the message of the text and thereby the ser-mon's primary affirmation. In some cases the mere re-reading of the biblical text may constitute an effective conclusion. Or the conclusion may be a restatement of the sermon's specific point as expressed in a Christian poem or in a great hymn of the church.

A word of caution is in order here, however. If the sermon-maker rarely has difficulty finding a hymn or poem to express the specific point of a sermon, it is likely that those sermons—unlike their texts—have no specific point. They may be expressing only some general biblical truth, rather than the specific truth of the text. There are many hymns and poems that articulate biblical truths. But there are many more specific truths and nuances found in biblical texts for which a hymn or poem has not yet been written. For example, so far as I know, no hymn or poem has ever reflected Paul's eschatological ethics, expressed in his admonition "let those who have wives live as though they had none, and those who mourn as though they were not mourning" (1 Cor. 7:29, 30). Again, it is possible to preach in a highly general way about faith and have no difficulty finding a hymn to serve as an apt conclusion. But how many hymns or poems express the distinctive teaching of Hebrews 11:1 that "faith is the assurance of things hoped for, the conviction of things not seen?" The more faithfully an expository sermon explicates its text, the more difficult it may be to discover a hymn or poem that can serve as an authentic conclusion for it.

The search for a hymn or poem that will serve the sermon's conclusion is, therefore, a moment of truth for the sermon-maker. If any number of hymns or poems appear serviceable, this very likely indicates that the sermon has proclaimed a biblical truth in a general way (as it would appear, for example, in a systematic theology or in a book on Christian doctrine) but not in the specific, unique way in which the text expresses it. A truly expository sermon must first, last, and always, from introduction to conclusion, be true to its text by being wholly governed by it, not by some generalized formulation of its truth. The sermon-maker who has no difficulty finding a hymn or poem to quote as an apt conclusion must ask whether that sermon has given notice to those peculiar nuances and dimensions of depth that characterize the text. On the other hand, difficulty in finding a hymn or poem that can serve as a conclusion to the sermon may be a tribute to the sermon-maker indicating a faithful explication of the distinctive teaching of the text.

A second word of caution. If the sermon-maker persistently finds it very difficult to construct a brief conclusion that reflects the content of the sermon, it is probable that the sermon lacks unity. As we have stressed over and again, a well-organized sermon explicates a single proposition. If this principle has been adhered to, there will be no special difficulty inherent in composing a brief concluding statement. But if the sermon has been only a running oral commentary on a number of successive verses in the Bible, giving attention to the explicit and implicit content of each verse, no brief recapitulation is possible. A sermon that makes many points will come to an end, but it will have no conclusion. Its end will owe more to the clock than to anything internal to the sermon. If the preacher cannot briefly summarize the thrust of the sermon at its end, it is likely that construction of that sermon occurred before there was discernment of the basic thrust of the text. An attempt has been made to speak God's Word before one has taken time to listen to that Word.

Most failures among preachers who fervently wish to proclaim the Word of God stem from this attempt to score many — rather than one — point in a sermon. To put it differently, such preachers should consider that just as the many verses of the Bible present the *one, single* Word of God, so the textually based sermon through its many words should announce the single, basic truth of its text. Every biblical text echoes the one divine Word, but none utters the whole Word in its fulness. Sermons should reflect this. Let them only give utterance to what their text declares — and not what other texts declare. Such sermons will reflect the unity that characterizes the biblical text and will present the text for what it is, one of many windows through which the richness and fulness of the divine Word is revealed. Such biblically based sermons will reflect and be shaped by that unity of the one Word heard in the multiplicity of biblical texts. Such sermons carry an inner unity that makes it relatively easy to construct conclusions for them.

The effectiveness of many sermons has been dulled and blunted by a preacher who did not know when to quit. When the real conclusion of the sermon is followed by one or more additional conclusions, it may mean that the preacher is more carried away by the sermon than are the hearers. Everyone who has been in the pulpit for any length of time knows the thrill (and the danger) of those new and exciting insights one suddenly sees into the meaning of the text—insights one did not see back in the study during preparation of the sermon. One must learn not to be carried away by such insightful and ecstatic moments. Multiple conclusions may also mean that the preacher is saying things which the text does not say, or is saying things which the text does say but which were left out of the body of the sermon because of his faulty and inadequate preparation.

Every aspect of sermon-making is hard work. But the sermon-maker who does not know how to conclude began too soon. The conclusion of the sermon is a moment of truth for the sermon-maker, for it is the moment when a discerning listener will discover whether the preacher kept the promise made in announcing the text.